Modern Critical Interpretations

George Bernard Shaw's
Man and Superman

Modern Critical Interpretations

These and other titles in preparation

Modern Critical Interpretations

George Bernard Shaw's
Man and Superman

Edited and with an introduction by
Harold Bloom
Sterling Professor of the Humanities
Yale University

714336

Chelsea House Publishers ◇ 1987
NEW YORK ◇ NEW HAVEN ◇ PHILADELPHIA

Library of Congress Cataloging-in-Publication Data
George Bernard Shaw's Man and superman.
    (Modern critical interpretations)
    Bibliography: p.
    Includes index.
    Contents: The theatre/Eric Bentley—Shaw/Louis
Kronenberger—Man and superman and the duel of sex/
Martin Meisel—[etc.]
    1. Shaw, Bernard, 1856–1950. Man and superman.
I. Bloom, Harold.   II. Title.   III. Series.
PR5363.M34G4   1987   822'.912   86–21573
ISBN 1-55546-028-3 (alk. paper)

Contents

Editor's Note

This book brings together a representative selection of the best criticism available upon George Bernard Shaw's *Man and Superman*. The critical essays are reprinted here in the order of their original publication. I am grateful to Daniel Klotz for his assistance in helping me to edit this volume.

My introduction analyzes the relationship of the play to Shaw's peculiar worship of the Life Force or Creative Evolution. Eric Bentley opens the chronological sequence by considering *Man and Superman* both as farce and meta-farce. In an exegesis of the play's relation to the inset drama, *Don Juan in Hell*, Louis Kronenberger centers on Don Juan's conceptions of Heaven and Hell, as does Frederick P. W. McDowell, with the difference that McDowell contextualizes the play in its historical moment of transition, from nineteenth- to twentieth-century London. Between Kronenberger and McDowell, Martin Meisel examines "the duel of sex" in the play, observing that Shaw, like Wilde, returned nineteenth-century stage comedy to something of Restoration verve and wit.

Louis Crompton, also centering upon *Don Juan in Hell*, regards it as "a classical philosophical dialogue," though modified by comic wit and high irony. Shavian spiritual autobiography, always prevalent in G. B. S., is traced in the play by Charles A. Berst, while Maurice Valency centers upon what might be called Shaw's own art of epistolary courtship.

Sally Peters Vogt emphasizes Ann Whitefield's archetypal role as Woman Incarnate, the origin and end of life, for Shaw. In this book's final essay, Nicholas Grene analyzes the Blakean dialectic of the play, showing that Shaw's excessive articulateness succeeds better as argument than as drama.

Introduction

"With the single exception of Homer there is no eminent writer, not even Sir Walter Scott, whom I despise so entirely as I despise Shakespear when I measure my mind against his." Shaw, obsessive polemicist, would write anything, even that unfortunate sentence. No critic would wish to measure Shaw's mind against Shakespeare's, particularly since originality was hardly Shaw's strength. Shavian ideas are quarried from Schopenhauer, Nietzsche, Ibsen, Wagner, Ruskin, Samuel Butler, Shelley, Carlyle, Marx (more or less), William Morris, Lamarck, Bergson—the list could be extended. Though an intellectual dramatist, Shaw essentially popularized the concepts and images of others. He continues to hold the stage and might appear to have earned his reputation of being the principal writer of English comic drama since Shakespeare. Yet his limitations are disconcerting, and the experience of rereading even his most famous plays, after many years away from them, is disappointingly mixed. They are much more than period pieces, but they hardly seem to be for all time. No single comedy by Shaw matches Wilde's *The Importance of Being Earnest* or the tragic farces of Beckett.

Eric Bentley best demonstrated that Shaw viewed himself as a prose prophet in direct succession to Carlyle, Ruskin, and Morris. This is the Shaw of the prefaces, of *Essays in Fabian Socialism,* of *Doctors' Delusions, Crude Criminology, Sham Education.* Only the prefaces to the plays are still read, and of course they are not really prefaces to the plays. They expound Shaw's very odd personal religion, the rather cold worship of Creative Evolution. Of this religion, one can say that it is no more bizarre than most and less distasteful than many, but it is still quite grotesque. To judge religions by aesthetic criteria may seem perverse, but what others are relevant for poems, plays, stories, novels, personal essays? By any aesthetic

1

standard, Shaw's heretical faith is considerably less interesting or impressive than D. H. Lawrence's barbaric vitalism in *The Plumed Serpent* or even Thomas Hardy's negative homage to the Immanent Will in *The Dynasts*.

G. K. Chesterton, in his book on Shaw (1909), observed that the heroine of *Major Barbara*

> ends by suggesting that she will serve God without personal hope, so that she may owe nothing to God and He owe everything to her. It does not seem to strike her that if God owes everything to her He is not God. These things affect me merely as tedious perversions of a phrase. It is as if you said, "I will never have a father unless I have begotten him."

"He who is willing to do the work gives birth to his own father," Kierkegaard wrote, and Nietzsche mused that "if one hasn't had a good father, then it is necessary to invent one." Shaw was neither a Darwinian nor a Freudian and I think he was a bad Nietzschean, who had misread rather weakly the sage of *Zarathustra*. But in his life he had suffered an inadequate father and certainly he was willing to do the work. Like his own Major Barbara, he wished to have a God who would owe everything to G. B. S. That requires a writer to possess superb mythopoeic powers, and fortunately for Shaw his greatest literary strength was as an inventor of new myths. Shaw endures in a high literary sense and remains eminently readable as well as actable because of his mythmaking faculty, a power he shared with Blake and Shelley, Wagner and Ibsen. He was not a stylist, not a thinker, not a psychologist, and utterly lacked even an iota of the uncanny Shakespearean ability to represent character and personality with overwhelming persuasiveness. His dialogue is marred by his garrulous tendencies, and the way he embodied his ideas is too often wearisomely simplistic. And yet his dramas linger in us because his beings transcend their inadequate status as representations of the human, with which he was hopelessly impatient anyway. They suggest something more obsessive than daily life, something that moves and has its being in the cosmos we learn to call Shavian, a comic version of Schopenhauer's terrible world dominated by the remorseless Will to Live.

As a critic, Shaw was genial only where he was not menaced, and he felt deeply menaced by the Aesthetic vision, of which his Socialism never quite got free. Like Oscar Wilde and Wilde's mentor Walter Pater, Shaw was the direct descendant of Ruskin, and his animus against Wilde and Pater reflects the anxiety of an ambitious son toward rival claimants to a heritage. Pater insisted upon style, as did Wilde, and Shaw has no style to speak of, not much more say than Eugene O'Neill. Reviewing Wilde's *An Ideal Husband* on January 12, 1895, for Frank Harris's *Saturday Review*, Shaw was both generous and just:

> Mr. Wilde, an arch-artist, is so colossally lazy that he trifles even with the work by which an artist escapes work. He distils the very quintessence, and gets as product plays which are so unapproachably playful that they are the delight of every playgoer with twopenn'orth of brains.

A month later, confronted by *The Importance of Being Earnest: A trivial comedy for serious people*, Shaw lost his composure, his generosity, and his sense of critical justice:

> I cannot say that I greatly cared for The Importance of Being Earnest. It amused me, of course; but unless comedy touches me as well as amuses me, it leaves me with a sense of having wasted my evening. I go to the theatre to be moved to laughter, not to be tickled or bustled into it; and that is why, though I laugh as much as anybody at a farcical comedy, I am out of spirits before the end of the second act, and out of temper before the end of the third, my miserable mechanical laughter intensifying these symptoms at every outburst. If the public ever becomes intelligent enough to know when it is really enjoying itself and when it is not, there will be an end of farcical comedy. Now in The Importance of Being Earnest there is plenty of this rib-tickling: for instance, the lies, the deceptions, the cross purposes, the sham mourning, the christening of the two grown-up men, the muffin eating, and so forth. These could only have been raised from the farcical plane by making them occur to characters who had, like Don Quixote, convinced us of their reality and obtained some hold on our sympathy. But that unfortunate moment of Gilbertism breaks our belief in the humanity of the play.

Would it be possible to have a sillier critical reaction to the most delightful comic drama in English since Shakespeare? Twenty three years later, Shaw wrote a letter (if it is that) to Frank Harris, published by Harris in his *Life of Wilde* (1918), and then reprinted by Shaw in his *Pen Portraits and Reviews*. Again Wilde was an artist of "stupendous laziness," and again was indicted, this time after his death, for heartlessness:

Our sixth meeting, the only other one I can remember, was the
one at the Café Royal. On that occasion he was not too preoc-
cupied with his danger to be disgusted with me because I, who
had praised his first plays handsomely, had turned traitor over
The Importance of Being Earnest. Clever as it was, it was his
first really heartless play. In the others the chivalry of the eighteenth century Irishman and the romance of the disciple of Théo-
phile Gautier (Oscar was old-fashioned in the Irish way, except
as a critic of morals) not only gave a certain kindness and gal-
lantry to the serious passages and to the handling of the women,
but provided that proximity of emotion without which laughter,
however irresistible, is destructive and sinister. In The Importance of Being Earnest this had vanished; and the play, though
extremely funny, was essentially hateful. I had no idea that Oscar
was going to the dogs, and that this represented a real degeneracy
produced by his debaucheries. I thought he was still developing;
and I hazarded the unhappy guess that The Importance of Being
Earnest was in idea a young work written or projected long
before under the influence of Gilbert and furbished up for Alex-
ander as a potboiler. At the Café Royal that day I calmly asked
him whether I was not right. He indignantly repudiated my
guess, and said loftily (the only time he ever tried on me the
attitude he took to John Gray and his more abject disciples) that
he was disappointed in me. I suppose I said, "Then what on
earth has happened to you?" but I recollect nothing more on
that subject except that we did not quarrel over it.

Shaw remains unique in finding *The Importance of Being Earnest* (of all
plays!) "essentially hateful." A clue to this astonishing reaction can be found
in Shaw's outraged response to Max Beerbohm's review of *Man and Superman,* as expressed in his letter to Beerbohm, on September 15, 1903:

You idiot, do you suppose I dont know my own powers? I tell
you in this book as plainly as the thing can be told, that the
reason Bunyan reached such a pitch of mastery in literary art
(and knew it) whilst poor Pater could never get beyond a nerve-
less amateur affectation which had not even the common workaday quality of vulgar journalism (and, alas! didnt know it,
though he died of his own futility), was that it was life or death
with the tinker to make people understand his message and see

his vision, whilst Pater had neither message nor vision & only wanted to cultivate style, with the result that of the two attempts I have made to read him the first broke down at the tenth sentence & the second at the first. Pater took a genteel walk up Parnassus: Bunyan fled from the wrath to come: that explains the difference in their pace & in the length they covered.

Poor Pater is dragged in and beaten up because he was the apostle of style, while Bunyan is summoned up supposedly as the model for Shaw, who also has a message and a vision. It is a little difficult to associate *The Pilgrim's Progress* with *Man and Superman,* but one can suspect shrewdly that Pater here is a surrogate for Wilde, who had achieved an absolute comic music of perfect style and stance in *The Importance of Being Earnest.* Shavians become indignant at the comparison, but Shaw does poorly when one reads side by side any of the *Fabian Essays* and Wilde's extraordinary essay "The Soul of Man Under Socialism." Something even darker happens when we juxtapose *Man and Superman* with *The Importance of Being Earnest,* but then Shaw is not unique in not being able to survive such a comparison.

II

Everything about *Man and Superman,* paradoxical as the play was to begin with, now seems almost absurdly problematical. The very title cannot mean (any more) what Shaw doubtless intended it to mean: the Superman of Nietzsche, Zarathustra, the heroic vitalist who prophesies the next phase of Creative Evolution, the next resting place of that cold God, the Life Force. Nietzsche's Zarathustra, as Shaw blandly chose never to see, is a god-man who is free of what Freud came to call the Over-I (superego), the shadow or spectre of bad conscience that hovers above each separate self. But Shaw's Superman is simply Bunyan's Pilgrim writ large and brought (supposedly) up to date, Shaw being about as much an immoralist as Bunyan.

Nietzsche transvalued all values (perhaps) or tried to (in some moods), and at the least developed an extraordinary perspectivism that really does call every stance—rhetorical, cosmological, psychological—into question. Shaw was interested neither in rhetoric (which he dismissed as Paterian "style") nor in psychology (Associationist or Freudian), and his cosmo-logical speculations, though mythologically powerful, are informed pri-marily by his post-Ruskinian and only quasi-Marxist political economics. His Fabian socialism marries the British Protestant or Evangelical sensibility

(Bunyan, Carlyle, Ruskin) to philosophical speculation that might transcend Darwinian-Freudian scientism (Schopenhauer, Lamarck, Nietzsche, Bergson). Such a sensibility is moral and indeed Puritanical, so that Shaw always remained in spirit very close to Carlyle rather than to Nietzsche (who despised Carlyle and loved Emerson for his slyly immoralistic Self-Reliance). Shaw's Superman, alas, in consequence looks a lot more like Thomas Carlyle crying out "Work, for the night cometh in which no man can work" than he does like Zarathustra-Nietzsche urging us: "Try to live as though it were morning."

In Shaw's defense, he took from the Nietzschean metaphor of the Superman what he most needed of it: a political and therefore literal reading, in which the Superman is nothing but what Shaw called "a general raising of human character through the deliberate cultivation and endowment of democratic virtue without consideration of property or class." That is a boring idealization, from an aesthetic or epistemological perspective, but pragmatically it is indeed what we most require and never will attain, which is why doubtless we must perish as a civilization. Such a consideration, fortunately, has nothing to do with *Man and Superman* as a farce and a sexual comedy, or with its glory, the extraordinary inserted drama of dialectic and mythology, *Don Juan in Hell*, certainly the outstanding instance of a play-within-a-play from Shakespeare to Pirandello.

The preface to *Man and Superman* is a dedicatory epistle to the drama critic Arthur Bingham Walkley and is a piece of Shavian outrageousness, particularly in promising far more than the play can begin to deliver. Shakespeare, perpetual origin of Shavian aesthetic anxiety, is associated with Dickens as being obsessed with the world's diversities rather than its unities. Consequently, they are irreligious, anarchical, nihilistic, apolitical, and their human figures are lacking in will. Against them, Shaw ranges Bunyan, Nietzsche and himself—the artist-philosophers! Shakespeare did not understand virtue and courage, which is the province of the artist-philosophers.

The shrewdest reply one could make to Shaw is to contrast Shakespeare's Falstaff (whom Shaw praises) to Nietzsche's Zarathustra. Which is the Superman, embodiment of the drive to live, person free of the superego? Hamlet, to Shaw, is an inadequate Don Juan, since he is famously irresolute. The sadness is that the Don Juan we will see debating the Devil in Hell is only (at best) a wistful impersonation of Hamlet, who remains the West's paradigm of intellectuality even as Falstaff abides forever as its paradigm of wit.

Yet this epistle commencing *Man and Superman* is one of Shaw's grandest performances, reminding us of how soundly he trained as a Hyde Park soapbox orator, a splendid preparation for a polemical playwright of ideas. In the midst of his perpetual advertisements for himself, he utters a poignant credo:

> Now you cannot say this of the works of the artist-philosophers. You cannot say it, for instance, of The Pilgrim's Progress. Put your Shakespearian hero and coward, Henry V and Pistol or Parolles, beside Mr Valiant and Mr Fearing, and you have a sudden revelation of the abyss that lies between the fashionable author who could see nothing in the world but personal aims and the tragedy of their disappointment or the comedy of their incongruity, and the field preacher who achieved virtue and courage by identifying himself with the purpose of the world as he understood it. The contrast is enormous: Bunyan's coward stirs your blood more than Shakespear's hero, who actually leaves you cold and secretly hostile. You suddenly see that Shakespear, with all his flashes and divinations, never understood virtue and courage, never conceived how any man who was not a fool could, like Bunyan's hero, look back from the brink of the river of death over the strife and labor of his pilgrimage, and say "yet do I not repent me"; or, with the panache of a millionaire, bequeath "my sword to him that shall succeed me in my pilgrimage, and my courage and skill to him that can get it." This is the true joy in life, the being used for a purpose recognized by yourself as a mighty one; the being thoroughly worn out before you are thrown on the scrap heap; the being a force of Nature instead of a feverish selfish little clod of ailments and grievances complaining that the world will not devote itself to making you happy. And also the only real tragedy in life is the being used by personally minded men for purposes which you recognize to be base. All the rest is at worst mere misfortune or mortality: this alone is misery, slavery, hell on earth; and the revolt against it is the only force that offers a man's work to the poor artist, whom our personally minded rich people would so willingly employ as pandar, buffoon, beauty monger, senti-mentalizer and the like.

Shakespeare then is not a prophet or at least does not himself suffer personally the burden of his prophecy. Bunyan and Shaw are prophets, and if they suffer, then also they experience the "true joy in life . . . the being a force of Nature." The passage has in it the accent of Carlyle, except that Carlyle rendered it with more gusto in his sublimely outrageous style, and Carlyle (not being in direct competition with Shakespeare) set Shakespeare first among the artist-prophets, higher even than Goethe. We are moved by Shaw, yet he has not the rhetorical power to overwhelm us (however dubiously) as Carlyle sometimes does.

Why has Shaw, of all dramatists, written a play about Don Juan Tenorio, or John Tanner, as he is called in *Man and Superman*? And in what way is the bumbling Tanner, cravenly fleeing the Life Force that is Ann Whitefield, a Don Juan? A crafty ironist, Shaw knows that all Don Juans, whether literary or experiential, are anything but audacious seducers. Poor Tanner is a relatively deliberate Shavian self-parody, and is all too clearly an Edwardian gentleman, a pillar of society, and very much a Puritan. He is all superego, and from the start is Ann's destined victim, her proper and inevitable husband, the father of her children. She will let him go on talking; she acts, and that is the end of it. The true Don Juan does not like women, which is why he needs so many of them. Tanner adores and needs Ann, though perhaps he will never know how early on the adoration and the need commenced in him.

Don Juan, as Shaw revises the myth, is Faust (whom Shaw calls the Don's cousin). He is the enemy of God, in direct descent from Faust's ancestor, Simon Magus the first Gnostic, who took the cognomen of Faustus ("the favored one") when he moved his campaign of charlatanry to Rome. Shaw's Don Juan is Prometheus as well as Faust, and so is an enemy not so much of God as of Jehovah (Shelley's Jupiter in *Prometheus Unbound*) the sky-tyrant, the deity of finance capitalism, repressive sexual morality, and institutional or historical Christianity.

It is manifest that *Man and Superman* does not have a Faustian or Promethean hero in the absurdly inadequate though amiable John Tanner. Tanner is, as Eric Bentley economically observes, a fool and a windbag, all-too-human rather than Don Juan Tenorio the Superman. But Shaw gives him a great dream: *Don Juan in Hell*. Again Bentley is incisive: "Take away the episode in hell, and Shaw has written an anti-intellectual comedy." I would go a touch further and say: "Take away the episode in hell, and Shaw has written a very unfunny comedy." Though it can be directed and acted effectively, most of the play singularly lacks wit; its paradoxes are sadly obvious. But the paradoxes of *Don Juan in Hell* continue to delight and disturb, as in the contrast between the erotic philosophies of Don Juan and the Statue:

DON JUAN: I learnt it by experience. When I was on earth, and
made those proposals to ladies which, though universally
condemned, have made me so interesting a hero of
legend, I was not infrequently met in some such way as
this. The lady would say that she would countenance my
advances, provided they were honorable. On inquiring
what that proviso meant, I found that it meant that I
proposed to get possession of her property if she had any,
or to undertake her support for life if she had not; that I
desired her continual companionship, counsel, and
conversation to the end of my days, and would take a
most solemn oath to be always enraptured by them:
above all, that I would turn my back on all other women
for ever for her sake. I did not object to these conditions
because they were exorbitant and inhuman: it was their
extraordinary irrelevance that prostrated me. I invariably
replied with perfect frankness that I had never dreamt of
any of these things; that unless the lady's character and
intellect were equal or superior to my own, her
conversation must degrade and her counsel mislead me;
that her constant companionship might, for all I knew,
become intolerably tedious to me; that I could not answer
for my feelings for a week in advance, much less to the
end of my life; that to cut me off from all natural and
unconstrained intercourse with half my fellowcreatures
would narrow and warp me if I submitted to it, and, if
not, would bring me under the curse of clandestinity;
that, finally, my proposals to her were wholly
unconnected with any of these matters, and were the
outcome of a perfectly simple impulse of my manhood
towards her womanhood.

ANA: You mean that it was an immoral impulse.

DON JUAN: Nature, my dear lady, is what you call immoral. I
blush for it; but I cannot help it. Nature is a pandar,
Time a wrecker, and Death a murderer. I have always
preferred to stand up to those facts and build institutions
on their recognition. You prefer to propitiate the three
devils by proclaiming their chastity, their thrift, and their
loving kindness; and to base your institutions on these

flatteries. Is it any wonder that the institutions do not
work smoothly?

THE STATUE: What used the ladies to say, Juan?

DON JUAN: Oh, come! Confidence for confidence. First tell me
what you used to say to the ladies.

THE STATUE: I! Oh, I swore that I would be faithful to the
death; that I should die if they refused me; that no
woman could ever be to me what she was—

ANA: She! Who?

THE STATUE: Whoever it happened to be at the time, my dear.
I had certain things I always said. One of them was that
even when I was eighty, one white hair of the woman I
loved would make me tremble more than the thickest
gold tress from the most beautiful young head. Another
was that I could not bear the thought of anyone else
being the mother of my children.

DON JUAN [revolted]: You old rascal!

THE STATUE [stoutly]: Not a bit; for I really believed it with all
my soul at the moment. I had a heart: not like you. And
it was this sincerity that made me successful.

DON JUAN: Sincerity! To be fool enough to believe a ramping,
stamping, thumping lie: that is what you call sincerity!
To be so greedy for a woman that you deceive yourself
in your eagerness to deceive her: sincerity, you call it!

THE STATUE: Oh, damn your sophistries! I was a man in love,
not a lawyer. And the women loved me for it, bless
them!

Does Shaw take sides? Don Juan, advance guard for the Superman,
presumably speaks for the dramatist, but our sympathies are divided, or
perhaps not called upon at all. I hear the stance of Shelley's *Epipsychidion*
taken up in Don Juan's rhetoric, probably as a deliberate allusion on Shaw's
part. The Statue though, splendid fellow, speaks the universal rhetoric of
all ordinary men in love, and his rather dialectical "sincerity" has its own
persuasiveness. Much trickier, and a larger achievement, is Shaw's man-
agement of the fencing-match between the Shavian Don Juan and that
Wildean-Paterian Aesthete, the Devil. Shaw's lifelong animus against Pater,
and his repressed anxiety caused by Wilde's genius as an Anglo-Irish comic
dramatist, emerge with authentic sharpness and turbulence as Don Juan and
the Devil face off. They are as elaborately courteous as Shaw and Wilde

always were with one another, but their mutual distaste is palpable, as
pervasive as the deep dislike of Shaw and Wilde for each other's works,
ideas, and personalities:

> THE DEVIL: None, my friend. You think, because you have a
> purpose, Nature must have one. You might as well
> expect it to have fingers and toes because you have them.
> DON JUAN: But I should not have them if they served no
> purpose. And I, my friend, am as much a part of Nature
> as my own finger is a part of me. If my finger is the
> organ by which I grasp the sword and the mandoline, my
> brain is the organ by which Nature strives to understand
> itself. My dog's brain serves only my dog's purposes; but
> my own brain labors at a knowledge which does nothing
> for me personally but make my body bitter to me and
> my decay and death a calamity. Were I not possessed
> with a purpose beyond my own I had better be a
> ploughman than a philosopher; for the ploughman lives
> as long as the philosopher, eats more, sleeps better, and
> rejoices in the wife of his bosom with less misgiving.
> This is because the philosopher is in the grip of the Life
> Force. This Life Force says to him "I have done a
> thousand wonderful things unconsciously by merely
> willing to live and following the line of least resistance:
> now I want to know myself and my destination, and
> choose my path; so I have made a special brain—a
> philosopher's brain—to grasp this knowledge for me as
> the husbandman's hand grasps the plough for me. And
> this" says the Life Force to the philosopher "must thou
> strive to do for me until thou diest, when I will make
> another brain and another philosopher to carry on the
> work."
> THE DEVIL: What is the use of knowing?
> DON JUAN: Why, to be able to choose the line of greatest
> advantage instead of yielding in the direction of the least
> resistance. Does a ship sail to its destination no better
> than a log drifts nowhither? The philosopher is Nature's
> pilot. And there you have our difference: to be in hell is
> to drift: to be in heaven is to steer.
> THE DEVIL: On the rocks, most likely.

DON JUAN: Pooh! which ship goes oftenest on the rocks or to the bottom? the drifting ship or the ship with a pilot on board?

THE DEVIL: Well, well, go your way, Señor Don Juan. I prefer to be my own master and not the tool of any blundering universal force. I know that beauty is good to look at; that music is good to hear; that love is good to feel; and that they are all good to think about and talk about. I know that to be well exercised in these sensations, emotions, and studies is to be a refined and cultivated being. Whatever they may say of me in churches on earth, I know that it is universally admitted in good society that the Prince of Darkness is a gentleman; and that is enough for me. As to your Life Force, which you think irresistible, it is the most resistable thing in the world for a person of any character. But if you are naturally vulgar and credulous, as all reformers are, it will thrust you first into religion, where you will sprinkle water on babies to save their souls from me; then it will drive you from religion into science, where you will snatch the babies from 'the water sprinkling and inoculate them with disease to save them from catching it accidentally; then you will take to politics, where you will become the catspaw of corrupt functionaries and the henchman of ambitious humbugs; and the end will be despair and decrepitude, broken nerve and shattered hopes, vain regrets for that worst and silliest of wastes and sacrifices, the waste and sacrifice of the power of enjoyment: in a word, the punishment of the fool who pursues the better before he has secured the good.

DON JUAN: But at least I shall not be bored. The service of the Life Force has that advantage, at all events. So fare you well, Señor Satan.

THE DEVIL [amiably]: Fare you well, Don Juan. I shall often think of our interesting chats about things in general. I wish you every happiness: heaven, as I said before, suits some people. But if you should change your mind, do not forget that the gates are always open here to the repentant prodigal. If you feel at any time that warmth of heart, sincere unforced affection, innocent enjoyment, and warm, breathing, palpitating reality.

This is hardly fair to the Devil, whose Paterian sense of repetition is a powerful answer to the Idealism of Schopenhauer's Life Force, and whose Ecclesiastes-like vision of vanity does not exclude the holiness of the heart's affections. Don Juan regards the Devil as a sentimentalist, but the Creative Evolution preached by the Shavian Don now seems precisely the sentimentality of a lost world. By a paradox that Shaw would not have enjoyed, the Aesthetic vision of Pater and Wilde now appears to be Ruskin's abiding legacy, while Shaw's Fabian Evolutionism would seem to have been a Ruskinian dead end. *Man and Superman* is effective enough farce, and its *Don Juan in Hell* is more than that, being one of the rare efforts to turn intellectual debate into actable and readable drama. Yet *Man and Superman* survives as theatre; if you want an artist-philosopher in social comedy, then you are better off returning to the sublime nonsense and Aesthetic vision of *The Importance of Being Earnest*, a play that Shaw so curiously condemned as being "heartless."

The Theatre

Eric Bentley

Shaw's first notable innovation in art was his creation of "unwomanly" heroines. (He once said that good women are all manly, "good men being equally all womanly men.") In his fight against the "romantic" love of popular fiction and drama Shaw showed that women are at once lower and higher than the fragile heroines of Dickens. They are lower because they lose their tempers like Blanche of *Widowers' Houses*. They are lower because their love is physical. Here is the first love scene in Shavian drama:

> They stand face to face . . . she provocative, taunting, half-defying, half-inviting him to advance, in a flush of undisguised animal excitement. It suddenly flashes on him that all this ferocity is erotic: that she is making love to him. His eyes light up: a cunning expression comes into the corner of his mouth.

Shavian heroines are also *higher* than Dickensian heroines. Higher, like Lady Cicely and Lina and Mrs George, in their superiority to erotics, in their naturalness and in their grandeur, in the nobility of their purpose and the effectiveness of their behaviour. Higher like Barbara and Jennifer and Lavinia and above all Joan in their soaring aspirations, their passion for realizing the ideal.

The relation between the sexes, throughout Shaw's works, has two levels. There is the famous Higher Relationship, which has given Shaw his reputation for sexlessness. The point of the *Three Plays for Puritans* was to show, in each play, a man and a woman with something larger than a

---

From *Bernard Shaw*. © 1975 by Eric Bentley. Proscenium Publishers, 1975.

romance on their hands. Read the plays closely, though, and you will see that this is no brushing-aside of sex by one who pretends to do without it. In each play—as we have noted—there is the shadow of a sex relationship between hero and heroine. Cupid, so to say, hovers over all six of them; his shadow is one of the subtlest and most interesting Shavian characters. In other plays there are many relationships which look "dangerous" but are not. In *Getting Married* and *The Apple Cart* Shaw replaces the eternal triangle with a Platonic triangle. In *Candida* and *The Devil's Disciple* adultery is held at arm's length with some difficulty. It is a wonder that Shaw escaped the charge of prurience.

For the most part the biological comedy is taken to be relatively low, the near-prurient spiritual comedy high. The one great exception is *Man and Superman*, in which the relation between the two levels is sought. It is a biological comedy with spiritual overtones, a spiritual comedy with a biological ground bass.

You would gather from the Epistle Dedicatory that *Man and Superman* has a world-shattering theme. A line of thought somewhat as follows—it is almost an anthropological myth—is expounded. Woman is the prime mover in the evolutionary process. While woman is creating and forming the race, man, needed only for a moment in the biological process, is left free to develop secondary interests, intellectual and social. Fearing to lose him, woman lures him back to domesticity by all possible means, among other things by a feigned interest in his intellectual and social pursuits.

This contest between the sexes we might call the lower biological comedy. Shaw indicates that a higher comedy—he calls it a tragedy—is enacted when the man is a genius and will not be led back to the woman. Unlike the ordinary straying male, a genius is not a truant from life. He escapes from the home only to fulfill as high a function of the Life Force as woman herself. For if woman preserves and creates life, genius is the means by which man becomes conscious of living. If he flees woman, his mother, he is the favourite child of his father, the Life Force. Without the woman there is no life, without him there is no value. When the artist man flees the mother woman, and the mother woman pursues the artist man, an irresistible force meets an immovable object.

Whether Shaw ever intended to present this "tragic" impasse in *Man and Superman* is not clear. He has certainly not done so. Tanner, as we have seen, cannot be regarded as an unequivocally great man. His appearance is a caricature of Hyndman. His behaviour is often that of a brilliant gasbag. A stage-direction describes Ann Whitefield as a "vital genius," but then we have to be careful to base our judgment of the play on the dialogue itself and not on Shaw's busy comments. Whatever his initial intention, Shaw has given us the lower biological comedy in which we have, not an impasse, not two irresistible forces, but the snapping-up of a clever young man by a shrewd young woman.

The Epistle Dedicatory contains some very big talk. It also sums up the play as "a trumpery story of modern London life, a life in which, as you know, the ordinary man's main business is to get means to keep up the position and habits of a gentleman and the ordinary woman's business is to get married." Turn to the play itself, resolutely ignore all its glittering adornments, and you will discover—among other things—a Victorian farce in four neatly arranged acts. The dialogue is of course interpenetrated with discussion. Not only is there abundant witticism on every possible topic. In each act, one main object of satire is added to the main story through the agency of extra characters—Ramsden the Liberal, Straker the New Man, Mendoza and his band of Radicals, Hector Malone, Sr., the Irish-American. Finally, Shaw uses the counterpoint of main plot and sub-plot. Ann begins by getting an inheritance and then spends her time landing a man. Violet begins by landing a man and then spends her time making sure she gets an inheritance too. Thus the two perennial comic themes—love and money—are treated with the perennial levity of farce.

And so *Man and Superman*, regarded by Shavians as a bible rivalling the "metabiological pentateuch" *Back to Methuselah*, regarded by anti-Shavians as a pompous bore, is—aside from the discussion in hell—a farce of the order of *You Never Can Tell*. In fact it looks back to the latter as much as it looks forward to the former. *You Never Can Tell* and *Man and Superman* sharpen Gilbertian satire to a finer edge than Gilbert himself ever gave it. I have in mind not only Mendoza's political pirates of Penzance but the fooling with family relationships that runs through both plays. With the exception of the opening of Becque's *La Parisienne* the story of Violet's marriage in act 1 of *Man and Superman* is probably the cleverest piece of histrionic deception in all modern comedy. To think of Bohun and his father William, of Mendoza and Louisa Straker (not to mention Guinness and Bill Dunn or the ancestry of Juggins) is to realize once again that Shaw had not been a Victorian theatre-goer for nothing.

We have seen how he raised his pseudo-melodramas above melodrama. How does he raise his pseudo-farce above farce? The most obviously unusual feature of the play viewed as a Victorian farce is—as one would expect—a Shavian inversion. The woman courts the man. But one learns also to expect that the primary simple inversion in a Shavian play is only the beginning of the irony. By giving an active sexual role to a woman

Shaw not only shocks the Victorians, he implements his own anthropological myth. More important, he broadens the whole basis of relations between the sexes as shown on the stage. "The natural attraction of the sexes" he presents as a physical, biological fact. Which is low and shocking. But the second irony is that this "lowness" is interpreted—and incontrovertibly—as "higher" than the conventional view, for what Ann Whitefield wants is not sexual pleasure but motherhood. *Man and Superman*, as I have said, is a fourth *Play for Puritans*.

Now in each *Play for Puritans* we [find] a protagonist standing for the Life Force and an antagonist who had against his will to be "educated" by the protagonist. According to the pattern, Tanner would be the protagonist, a role he seems to be well fitted for by his creed, his knowledge, his eloquence, and his pedagogical passion. He poses as the veritable high priest of the Life Force. But in *Man and Superman*, as in *Pygmalion* later, protagonist and antagonist are reversed. Though Tanner *preaches* the Life Force, Ann *is* the Life Force. In the end he goes to school to her. If the play has the standard Shaw theme of vitality versus system, its upshot is that the apostle of vitality is himself the slave of system, for like other doctrines vitalism can lose its vitality. Tanner is system, Ann spontaneous life.

If *Man and Superman* is far from containing the tragedy mentioned in the Epistle, it also rises far above the farce that is its basis. Nor is the tragic theme altogether ignored. It is not the Epistle but the play that contains the sentence: "Of all human struggles there is none so treacherous and remorseless as the struggle between the artist man and the mother woman." But though the "mother woman" who inspired the sentence is Ann Whitefield, the "artist man" here referred to is the poet Octavius, who in reality is not much of an artist and even less of a man. The speaker—the impartial observer!—is Tanner, who is not an artist but a political theorist. What is Shaw doing with his tragic idea? Is he not looking at it slantwise, shyly declining to use it? It might be said that Tanner is more of an artist in the Shavian sense than Octavius, as Caesar is more of an artist than Apollodorus. But is he? Is he?—not as an idea in a preface but as an actuality in the play? The destiny that Ann and Tanner work out is precisely that of the lower biological comedy. Tanner's intellectual pretensions shrink to nothing before Ann's reality. Tanner is brought to heel precisely as Shaw says the genius is not.

Octavius is not a genius either. Those who think all Shaw's artists the same have compared him with Marchbanks. But Marchbanks probably *was* a genius, though, at the beginning, an immature one. Marchbanks would have seen through Tanner, and would have placed himself as an immovable object in the way of Ann, had she exerted upon him her irresistible force. There is a play in this, but Shaw did not write it. His artists—for that matter it is true of most of his people, "typical" as they are—never exactly duplicate each other. Octavius is isolated like Marchbanks, but for him isolation is frankly a *pis aller*. The triangle Dick-Judith-Anderson was different from the triangle Marchbanks-Candida-Morell, and the triangle Octavius-Ann-Tanner is different again. In all of them Shaw touches some very delicate springs. His central situation is crude but here on the margin is something subtle and mysterious. Those who are disappointed that Shaw did not attempt a Strindbergian tragedy of love can find some compensations in his equally curious triangular tragi-comedies.

Shaw

Louis Kronenberger

Man and Superman is, of course, one of Shaw's major plays, though it perhaps achieves that rank from being not one play, but two. Certainly without the long third-act dialogue in Hell, *Man and Superman*—for all that it dramatizes the best known of Shaw's theories—would diminish into one of his more tractable and traditional comedies. With the Hell scene, it expands into one of the most brilliant and Shavian of them.

Yet to speak of *Man and Superman* as two plays is not quite happy, either. The whole thing is more like a pleasant three-course comedy dinner, with an interruption—between meat course and dessert—in the form of a long dazzling dialectical floor show. The scene in Hell tremendously sharpens and complicates and enriches the rest of the story, but it is a dialogue merely, far more akin to several of Shaw's own prefaces than to *any* man's third act, and most akin of all to something like Diderot's equally brilliant dialogue, *Rameau's Nephew.* So that one is not merely metaphorical in treating act 3 of *Man and Superman* as interpolated fireworks and acts 1, 2, and 4 as ordinary comedy fare. The two things are related without being, really, interdependent: it is no offense against art to offer the play without the Hell scene, and it is all in all in the interests of art to offer the Hell scene without the play.

In any case Shaw deals here, in one of the most famous of his comedies, with one of the most famous of all theater courtships—a courtship that owes its fame to the fact that the woman is shown to do the courting. This

From *The Thread of Laughter: Chapters on English Stage Comedy from Jonson to Maugham* © 1952 and renewed 1980 by Louis Kronenberger. Alfred A. Knopf, 1952.

has quite as much value as sheer entertainment as it could ever have as sexual biology; and the spectacle of demure Ann Whitefield plotting with all her strength to nab hardheaded, unconventional John Tanner is amusing enough, and has possibilities enough, simply as farce. She professes to be the most daughterly of girls, to want only to do what would please her dead father, were he alive. Actually she has seen to it that her father's will should have designated John Tanner one of her guardians—as the most practicable way of eventually making him her husband. Beyond that she tells the most barefaced lies, she goes in for the most flagrant hypocrisies— with her mother, with her guardian, with the man she *doesn't* want quite as much as with the man she does. And John recognizes the lies, and upbraids her. And sees through the hypocrisies, and denounces her. And, thanks to his chauffeur, perceives that she is pursuing him—and runs away from her. But she overtakes him in his flight, and he is once again face to face with her. And her sexual lure overwhelms not only him, but even all that he knows about her, and he marries her.

That is the story—which is to say, that is how any ordinarily competent light-comedy ironist would have viewed the situation, positing that no man is smart or strong-willed enough to escape a really determined woman whom he happens to find sexually attractive. And though Shaw has much to say on other subjects in *Man and Superman*, on *this* subject he hasn't, in the end, much more to say than the ordinary competent writer of light comedy. Shaw, to be sure, brings in the Life Force; and Shaw ultimately identifies the Life Force with humanity's upward striving rather than its intersexual strife. But in *Man and Superman* (the three-act play) Shaw's Life Force seems little more than what the old poets would have termed Nature, or at most the desire to carry on and improve the race. The Life Force is here, at least, something that can swamp the reason and defeat the will, something that can even rattle Shaw, and convert so great a champion of rationality to a kind of mysticism.

Philosophically, we may allow that Shaw's Life Force—if only because it *is* so instinctive a force, or metaphysical a process—might, for argument's sake, exist. But theatrically, in the case of *Man and Superman*, Shaw's Life Force, rather more than it is Bergson's *élan vital* or Shakespeare's plain nature or your mating instinct or my desire to carry on and improve the race—theatrically, Shaw's Life Force here seems more than half our old friend, the god from the machine. It requires the Life Force at its most compelling to get Tanner to marry Ann. For the facts simply don't permit us to regard Tanner as the mere male who is no match for the scheming female. The whole basis of that theory is that the male isn't on to the female, or at least to *all* of her, that he interprets her aggressiveness as solicitude, that he supposes the ideas she plants in him to have grown there of themselves. Or he knows the worst about women, but finds his own woman an exception; or he is portrayed as an idealist, or an idiot, or ripe for plucking, or catchable on the rebound. Tanner, however, is not only in the general sense a very emancipated and extremely unsentimental man; he also knows exactly what Ann is up to: how deviously she conspires, how ruthlessly she pursues. He has every reason to dislike and distrust her, and Shaw—to make his point—has to make Ann somebody we dislike and distrust as well. Nor is Tanner presented as head over heels in love with the girl and powerless to resist her. For argument's sake, one may concede that she attracts him more than he will allow. But that is still not enough of an argument: the Life Force simply overpowers Tanner so that Shaw can make his point and have his joke, as some god from the machine appears in a more usual kind of play so that the author can round off his plot. The psychology behind Tanner would be more convincing if we treated him as ruefully resigned to marrying the determined Ann rather than unable to resist her; if he, quite as much as the audience, relished the irony of his situation; if, tied up with this transcendental mating instinct there were just a touch of a martyr complex.

Fortunately the Ann–Tanner relationship is not the only one that counts in *Man and Superman*. There are, in terms of subplot, Violet's marriage to Malone, and in terms of byplay, Tanner's relations with Straker. The matter of Violet Robinson, who we are led to believe is quite brazenly about to become a mother without having become a wife, is in Shaw's best prankish manner; for after milking the situation for all it is worth, and having all kinds of people react in all kinds of ways, Shaw lets Violet indignantly reveal that, of course, she's married. As for Tanner's relationship with Straker, though it seems more traditional than the joke about Violet seems pat, actually it has a good deal about it that is—or that once was—new. And what is new about the relationship is what is new about Straker, who is not just the resourceful, impertinent servant found in comedy of every age and nation, but the servant who has become educated and intellectually enlightened. A chauffeur or mechanic today, Straker will be an engineer or inventor tomorrow. In caste terms, he is of course still a cockney, and in cultural terms, which is more significant, he is still an outsider—for education does not quite mean culture, any more than birth means breeding. But that is by the way: the point is that Straker can not only, like a dozen Figaros, tell his master that Ann is set to have him; like no Figaro, when Tanner ascribes a quotation to Voltaire, he can say, oh no, it's from Beaumarchais. Intellectually Straker can talk Tanner's language, even though he still lacks his enunciation.

All this is good enough Shavian philosophy and Shavian fooling, but it operates at a different level, and for that matter in a literally quite different world, from the third-act scene in Hell. The Hell scene is only technically a part of the play. Indeed, it can only very doubtfully be regarded as playwriting; but that is of no importance, for nowhere in English during the twentieth century has there been a more dazzlingly sustained discussion of ideas in dialogue form. The Hell scene is a great blaze of fireworks and something more than fireworks, even if of something less than clear intellectual light. The scene, which is a dream scene, contains four characters: Don Juan Tenorio, not only Mozart's and Molière's and Shadwell's and history's and legend's libertine, but John Tanner's ancestor: Doña Ana, whose descendant or double is Ann Whitefield; Doña Ana's father, the Commendatore whom Don Juan slew; and the Devil. None of these people is at all as we last met him elsewhere, nor is Hell or Heaven at all like what others have painted them. The Devil is not much of a surprise: as in his earthly appearances he is extremely eager to tempt, so in his own country he is exceedingly eager to please. He is rather like the owner of a resort hotel trying to dangle before the better type of guest the very best type of entertainment. He is much helped by the fact that, though Heaven has all the prestige of a Newport, it displays all the dullness of Old Point Comfort. Hell is indeed a home for the escapists, the pleasure-seekers, the reality-shunners, for those whose lives, conceived in frivolousness, have on earth gone unfulfilled. It is an ideal place for living an animal existence on a non-physical basis: where, that is to say, one can always be as young and look as young and act as young as one chooses, unmenaced by the ravages of Time. Shaw's Hell is a sort of vulgar idea of Heaven. There has been a great deal of switching over from the real Heaven; Ana's statue father, the Commendatore, a military man of worldly tastes and conservative values, has just come down from Heaven, leaving a forwarding address in Hell.

Ana, perhaps the most famous of the ladies whom Juan betrayed, has recently died and is incensed to find that she has been relegated to Hell. She is incensed even more to find that her father has turned his back on Heaven; indeed she is appalled in a great number of ways—as a wronged woman sent to the afterworld for wrongdoers; as a religious woman abandoned to the Devil; as a wifely and motherly woman thrust into a pit of courtesans and strumpets. She insists that Heaven be her reward, whether or not it turn out rewarding. Better to yawn in Heaven than whoop things up in Hell: though Doña Ana is quite sure that Heaven must be very agreeable.

It is Shaw's Don Juan who is most purely, most drastically Shavian. First of all, his reputation as a heartless rake and libertine is an ill-founded one: he kept running away from women because he found them getting possessive, not because, having possessed them, he found them getting dull. He ran away out of fear and in self-defense, exactly as John Tanner ran away from Ann Whitefield. He accordingly renounced the flesh, and he means now to reject the Devil. He believes in the brain, which alone distinguishes man from the brute, and by means of which man may, in time, evolve the superman. The Devil attempts to answer him:

> And is Man any the less destroying himself for all this boasted brain of his? Have you walked up and down upon the earth lately? I have; and I have examined Man's wonderful inventions. And I tell you that in the arts of life Man invents nothing; but in the arts of death he outdoes Nature herself, and produces by chemistry and machinery all the slaughter of plague, pestilence, and famine. The peasant I tempt today eats and drinks what was eaten and drunk by the peasants of ten thousand years ago. . . . But when he goes out to slay, he carries a marvel of mechanism that lets loose at the touch of his finger all the hidden molecular energies, and leaves the javelin, the arrow, the blowpipe of his fathers far behind. In the arts of peace Man is a bungler . . . I know his clumsy typewriters and bungling locomotives and tedious bicycles: they are toys compared to the Maxim gun, the submarine torpedo boat . . . Man measures his strength by his destructiveness.

Don Juan has his answer for this:

> Your weak side, my diabolic friend, is that you have always been a gull: you take Man at his own valuation. Nothing would flatter him more than your opinion of him. He loves to think of himself as bold and bad . . . Call him tyrant, murderer, pirate, bully; and he will adore you . . . Call him liar and thief; and he will only take an action against you for libel. But call him coward; and he will go mad with rage: he will face death to outface that stinging truth.

Don Juan is going to Heaven—the Exchange Plan works both ways— precisely because it is not for those who are forever seeking happiness, but because it is for those who will work and strive, who will face and become the masters of reality. Shaw's Heaven is a Puritan's Heaven where the Life Force can operate with benign efficiency (and in the Hell scene the Life

Force approximates a kind of spiral movement upward, during which man sheds everything physical except his wings). It guides the one kind of man who, Don Juan says, "has ever been happy, has ever been universally respected"—the philosophic man. For Woman, Juan confesses, there was much to be said: through her he obtained not only amorous but much esthetic pleasure. What spoiled it all was that whenever he took happy leave of women, they murmured "When will you come again?" Since that meant falling into their clutches, it constituted the signal for running away, and he was asked the question so often, and ran away so often, that he became famous for running away—or, as Doña Ana puts it, infamous. The wrangling between Juan and Ana has its share of good things, as when Juan says to her: "I say nothing against your chastity, Señora, since it took the form of a husband and twelve children. What more could you have done had you been the most abandoned of women?"—and she answers, "I could have had twelve husbands and no children."

There is a good deal of point to the revision of ideas and reversal of values that go not only with Shaw's conception of Don Juan, but equally with Don Juan's conception of Hell and Heaven. Juan's heaven is rather the headquarters of progress than the seat of perfection; a celestial workshop and meeting hall rather than a final abode of the blest. And the demonstration—or at any rate the dialectics—is brilliant. If Juan himself is more than a little windy, the general effect—as language, as wit, as paradox, as repartee, as intellectual gymnastics—is extraordinary. If there is a weakness, it is that Juan and Juan's Heaven and Hell can only be startlingly unorthodox as the cost of being uncommonly improbable. In turning accepted ideas inside out, the problem is always to provide something that seems challenging without seeming false. Sir Osbert Sitwell has recently told the story of Cinderella, in which Cinderella comes off a prig with a martyr fixation, whose stepsisters talk themselves blue in the face trying to get her to come out of the scullery. That idea is both amusing and conceivable, and so is Shaw's that Don Juan did not abandon women from boredom, but ran away from them out of fear. But even the fact that he ran away from so many of them does not acquit him of first approaching them out of sexual desire: he may not have been the profligate of legend, but even less does he seem a Puritan like Shaw. Almost the reverse psychology would be sounder, I think: had Juan really been a libertine leading an altogether self-indulgent life of the flesh, he might so much have had his fill of sex on earth as to seek something almost immoderately spiritual in Heaven. And if the answer is that in that case he would have been a sinner and ineligible for Heaven, the counterreply is that anyone is eligible for Shaw's Heaven— the point being that almost no one is eager for it. In strict logic, Heaven for Juan would be—among other things, at least—a place where beautiful and obliging ladies merely said "*Au revoir*" instead of "When will you come again?"

As for Heaven and Hell, though they need not be conventional abodes of bliss and suffering, it is hard to accept them on the terms offered by Shaw. I mean this less as a matter of morality than as a matter of taste. Shaw's Hell, though a place of pleasure rather than pain, remains morally sound because its inhabitants are shown to be second-rate—shoddy, spineless, pleasure-seeking. All the same, one is not much tempted by the spectacle of Shaw's Heaven, and for that matter, one is not much convinced. One could easily accept it as high-thinking and plain-living viewed as an end in itself—for the severity of that idea possesses real moral grandeur. But Juan's Heaven has a real odor of uplift and the social worker about it, a sense, in fact, of preparation for a still higher life to come. There aren't many things to insist on as basic requirements for Heaven, but surely one of them is that it should be more than a mere way station, a mere rung on a ladder. And the real reason for its not being is that Shaw's Life Force remains valid only as long as it remains evolutionary, as it continues to strive and progress; once it achieves its goal, not only has it no further reason to exist, but the Superman it has brought into existence would seem peculiarly lacking in personal—or even identifiable—qualities. Shaw's Superman would be at most a vibration in a void.

The brilliance of the Hell scene is thus a trifle self-defeating: the whole thing is a kind of triumph of Shaw over sense, and *any* triumph over sense must smack partly of failure. On a serious plane, Shaw is at once too doctrinaire about the Life Force and too vague about what it culminates in, just as when he isn't making sport of Heaven he is rather too solemn about it. But perhaps the main trouble with his brilliance here is that it is progressively at the expense of each of his characters and of all of their ideas: they kill one another off, they cancel one another out—which makes for very good comedy, but quite doubtful "constructive" thinking. One can only end as one began, by saying that the Hell scene is a very grand-scale and long-drawn-out display of fireworks. This whole dazzling side is, indeed, its magnificent merit; its doctrinaire side is its rather considerable weakness. Don Juan is jockeyed into being a mouthpiece for Shaw just as John Tanner is jockeyed into being a mate for Ann; they have no choice; the Life Force has about it more than a touch of *force majeure*; the superman, at several removes from Nietzsche's *Übermensch*, bears the stamp of Shaw himself. But the scene's defects of logic, its perversities of argument, can at worst only shrivel it to a mere triumph of wit.

Man and Superman and the Duel of Sex

Martin Meisel

The duel of sex was not common in nineteenth-century English comedy before Wilde and Shaw. However, in its long decline from its Restoration dominance, it never altogether disappeared; it simply became less witty, less verbal, more at home in farce than in courtship comedy. Where it survives in the nineteenth century with some suggestion of its old flavor, there is usually some exceptional circumstance. For example, it survives in Boucicault's *London Assurance* (1841), a play which in many respects of style and theme belongs to the eighteenth century. It survives in H. T. Craven's *Meg's Diversion* (1866), on condition that the duellists are not the destined lovers. It survives in S. Theyre Smith's *My Uncle's Will* (1870), where the stakes are not sexual conquest and marriage, but the gain or loss of an inheritance. It survives finally in the comedies of James Sheridan Knowles, in consequence of their debt to Shakespeare; so that in *The Love Chase* (1837) there is an obvious Beatrice and Benedick couple, Constance and Wildrake, who plague each other endlessly until Trueworth maneuvers a discovery of mutual love and a match. (There is also a sentimental couple, Young Waller and Lydia, a ladies' maid who meets Waller's attempts to seduce her with stiff resistance and honorable love until, hopelessly out-generalled, he is reduced to marriage, and is assuaged with the discovery that the maid is really a lady.)

Implicit in the sex duel is the woman's desire to have the man on her own terms. In nineteenth-century farcical comedy, this becomes the re-

---

From *Shaw and the Nineteenth-Century Theater.* © 1963 by Princeton University Press.

versed love chase. Shaw suggests Shakespeare's aggressive heroines as his antecedents for the pursuit in *Man and Superman*; but after *The Wild Goose Chase* the situation is a stock motif, though in the nineteenth century it seems to have dropped out of "serious" comedy. It appears, however, in Gilbert's farces and burlesques, in his race of middle-aged maiden contraltos, and in such heroines as Caroline Effingham in *Tom Cobb* (1875), who, resorting to breach of promise proceedings, kneels at Tom's feet *"kissing his hand as she places the writ in it."* The reversed love chase appears in more characteristic form in Charles Selby's "Musical Interlude" *The Bonnie Fish Wife* (1858), in which Miss Thistledown disguises herself as Maggie Mac-farline, a fishwife, in order to lure and catch Wildoats Heartycheer, the young blade who fled from her as the bride designated by his father. Tom Taylor's "Comedietta" *Nine Points of the Law* (1859) tells how the widow, Mrs. Smylie, uses her wit and artfulness to secure both a cottage whose title is in dispute and a good husband. The widow is far cleverer and more determined than any male character, most of whom patronize and "protect" her, or pretend to. Candida, Ann Whitefield, and, to some extent, Lady Cicely Waynflete are Shaw's women in this line.

Shaw presents straightforward instances of the reversed love chase in *The Philanderer, Man and Superman, Misalliance, The Village Wooing*, and *The Millionairess*, and it is undoubtedly his most common dramatic approach to the relation between the sexes. In *Misalliance* he shows the heroine actually chasing her prey off stage, and then being chased by him back on. In *The Philanderer* and its complement, *You Never Can Tell*, the duel of sex is revived in terms of modern movements and the New Woman. Despite his name, the Philanderer, like Shaw's Don Juan, is more pursued than pursuing, but he uses the new fashions to win the duel and evade capture successfully. Valentine, "the Duellist of sex" in *You Never Can Tell*, also like Shaw's Don Juan, is caught when a force beyond himself, a Life Force in fact, seizes him in the midst of flirtation and sweeps him into marriage.

In *Major Barbara* Shaw uses conventions of the love chase, but transposed to another key. Though the drum-carrying Cusins is "the very unusual *jeune premier* of the play" his pursuit of Barbara gives way for a time to her pursuit of Bill Walker. In a note to the American press on the production of *Major Barbara*, Shaw wrote, "The possibility of using the wooing of a man's soul for his salvation as a substitute for the hackneyed wooing of a handsome young gentleman for the sake of marrying him had occurred to Bernard Shaw many years before." And though Bill Walker belongs to the line Dickens distilled into Bill Sikes, Shaw insisted on another occasion that he was not to look "like a murderer in a nightmare or melodrama. He should be clean and good looking enough to make the scene in which Barbara breaks down his brutality—which is a sort of very moving love scene—look natural, which it will not do if Bill is disgusting physically and sanitarily." It is this hidden ground of the love chase which should make Barbara's passion over the loss of Bill's soul emotionally convincing to the audience.

In *Man and Superman, A Comedy and a Philosophy,* the reversed love chase is the governing action of the entire play. In keeping with its nineteenth-century farcical associations, the chase is given a most literal physical embodiment in a motorized race across Europe. In the first act, the audience is made elaborately acquainted with the antagonists and with the chase as it proceeds in its covert stages. John Tanner, the descendant of Don Juan Tenorio, even inflicts a mild defeat on Ann, his pursuer, by his persistent unconsciousness in their flirtation. But in the second act, Tanner is enlightened by his less visionary chauffeur and the literal stage of the chase begins. The act builds to a striking close written in the vein of melodramatic farce and, for sensational realistic effect with the latest thing (in 1903), worthy of a Dion Boucicault or an Augustus Harris. An automobile planted before the eyes of the audience through the entire act spectacularly drives off the stage.

Some of the apparent paradoxical novelty in *Man and Superman* arose from Shaw's invocation of the Don Juan legend and his presentation of the arch-pursuer of all time as (in modern dress) the arch-pursued. Actually, Mozart and Da Ponte were beforehand in this respect, and a shrewd observer such as Max Beerbohm was more impressed by the obvious conventionality of *Man and Superman* than by its seeming novelty: "Mr. Shaw, using art merely as a means of making people listen to him, naturally lays hands on the kind that appeals most quickly to the greatest number of people. There is something splendid in the contempt with which he uses as the vehicle for [his] thesis a conventional love-chase, with motors and comic brigands thrown in. He is as eager to be a popular dramatist and as willing to demean himself in any way that may help him to the goal, as was (say) the late Mr. Pettitt [one of the leading writers of hack melodrama]."

There is an essential relationship, however, between Shaw's conventional love chase and his thesis, so that he might have argued with Beerbohm that, far from demeaning himself with the love chase, he alone had managed to give it its proper philosophical due. In Shaw's creative-evolutionary philosophy, the love chase became a metaphor for the relation of male and female principles in the universe. In the detachable third act of *Man and Superman,* John Tanner becomes his ancestor Don Juan, the male principle, the projective imagination of the Life Force. [Ann Whitefield becomes Doña Ana, the female principle, the generative vital instinct. Both are ruthless in their way, and their appearance in the third act establishes a cosmic theater for the combat and love chase of Tanner and Ann.]In the epistle which prefaces the play Shaw offers his rationale for his translation of the sex duel, the love combat between men and women to have each other on their own terms, into the impersonal and universal:

> We observe in the man of genius all the unscrupulousness and all the "self-sacrifice" (the two things are the same) of Woman. He will risk the stake and the cross; starve, when necessary, in a garret all his life; study women and live on their work and care as Darwin studied worms and lived upon sheep; work his nerves into rags without payment, a sublime altruist in his disregard of himself, an atrocious egotist in his disregard of others. Here Woman meets a purpose as impersonal, as irresistible as her own; and the clash is sometimes tragic.

The results of the clash in *Man and Superman* are conventionally comic rather than tragic. With the help of brigands, Ann's car catches Tanner's in the mountains of the Sierra Nevada, and in Granada she brings him to bay: *"He makes an irresolute movement towards the gate; but some magnetism in her draws him to her, a broken man."* From this point, though the struggle rises to an intense climax, Tanner cooperates in his own defeat: "The Life Force. I am in the grip of the Life Force." When Ann nears exhaustion and loses her courage to go on, Tanner insists on continuing the struggle. When she compromises him by declaring "I have promised to marry Jack," he says aside to his friend and rival Tavy, "I never asked her. It is a trap for me"; but he never says so publicly.

In the last encounter Shaw gives a vitalist impersonality to the conflict. Much talk of the Life Force, Tanner's behavior even in embracing Ann as if he were in the grip of an electric current, Ann's behavior as if she were undergoing the pains of birth, all contribute to the sense of extra-personality. The forces involved in the conventional duel of sex are made explicit, and it is made quite plain that there is an ambivalence in the happiness of the conventional comedy ending. Marriage for Tanner, the ineluctably free male spirit and man of creative intellect, is biological subjection, is "apostasy, profanation of the sanctuary of my soul, violation of my manhood, sale of my birthright, shameful surrender, ignominious capitulation, acceptance of defeat." But both sides of the inherent ambivalence of the conventional ending are essential parts of its philosophical usefulness, its functioning as a philosophical metaphor. The lover's defeat is also a victory and an occasion for happiness; and the marriage ending of *Man and Superman* is an emblem of the ultimate identity of the two aspects of the Life Force: its generative vital impulse and its projective intellectual aspiration to knowledge of itself. The genre conventions of the comedy of romance and courtship were generally useful to Shaw as theatrical points of departure and sources of dramatic appeal; but in *Man and Superman* the two chief characters in one of the basic relationships of the genre are raised to symbolic significance, so that the Comedy becomes a parable for a Philosophy.

Heaven, Hell, and
Turn-of-the-Century London

Frederick P. W. McDowell

Some years before Shaw wrote *Man and Superman* he had asserted that the only immoral feature of Mozart's *Don Giovanni* was its "supernatural retributive morality." Don Giovanni—like Don Juan and Jack Tanner—breaks through "the ordinary categories of good and evil" to achieve a new morality. The world, in fact, may well owe more, Shaw said, to its Don Juans—its defiers of convention and its enemies of supernatural, theological, and moral authority—than to its Don Ottavios. Certainly in terms of Shaw's play the world would scarcely owe anything to Octavius Robinson, while Jack Tanner is a quickening voice, a prophet crying in the wilderness, an enthusiastic and energetic theoretician of reform. In a notice written before *Man and Superman* Shaw presented Nietzsche as a devil's advocate of the modern type who rejects the "duty, morality, law, and altruism" exalted by the party of convention above faith. In the play Jack Tanner and Don Juan are spokesmen of faith, in environments that favor conventionality or, what is worse, a gentlemanly skepticism. Each in his iconoclasm would support Shaw's valuation in the Epistle Dedicatory of "the career of the conventionally respectable and sensible Worldly Wiseman as [being] no better at bottom than the life and death of Mr. Badman." Each rejects the tyranny of received opinion, Don Juan the religious and moral conventions of a feudal society such as duty, honor, and justice; Jack Tanner the "forces of middle class public opinion . . . now triumphant everywhere."

Jack Tanner feels that the prescriptive standards of the upper middle class derive from a morality deficient in vitality and sympathy. He hastens

---

From *Drama Survey* 2, no. 3 (February 1963). © 1963 by *Drama Survey*.

to defend Violet Robinson when she is pregnant, supposedly with an illegitimate child; and he congratulates Hector Malone on his defiance of existing standards when the latter dares to love the woman he has been attracted to though she is already married. Even if Tanner's instincts are just, his sympathies in both instances are misplaced. The people he defends observe all the proprieties and resent Tanner's assumption that they could have been guilty of "immoral" or "advanced" behavior. Violet is, of course, married to Hector (though the identity of the husband is until act 4 known only to the audience), and the married woman Hector has made love to is his own wife.

Tanner again attacks conventional standards when he derides familial obligations to Ann in act 2, especially the subservience of the child to the parent of the opposite sex. Jack's tone is similar when in act 4 he declares to Mrs. Whitefield that parents need not admire their children just because they are their children: "I suspect that the tables of consanguinity have a natural basis in a natural repugnance." For Tanner the critical scrutiny of current attitudes is more important in family relationships than the law of love. For Tanner too many of his contemporaries are like Octavius Robinson. In Violet's "trouble" he should be thinking of her necessities, Jack alleges, rather than of his own principles and of other people's reactions to her "disgrace." Our workaday morality, says Jack, in answer to Roebuck Ramsden's attack upon him at this point, has as its father the Devil. Jack speaks figuratively here, but the metaphor turns out to be an actuality when we remember the Devil's adulation of imposing but worn-out absolutes.

In the Devil's realm universals like "beauty, purity, respectability, religion, morality, art, patriotism, bravery, and the rest" are mere words. If they were actualities, the Devil would be out of business since meaningless abstractions would no longer pass current for moral concepts. As it is, they are words, slogans, formulas, "useful for duping barbarians into adopting civilization, or the civilized poor into submitting to be robbed and enslaved." On the other hand, for our spiritual regeneration, we need to recover a true sense of beauty, purity, patriotism and the rest; accompanying Tanner's birth of "moral passion" as a boy was just this sense that veracity and honor had now become meaningful entities instead of catchwords. In their debased form in hell the absolutes of tradition have become pernicious because they are shams masquerading as eternal verities. With respect to sex, Don Juan declares that virtue is confused with a social institution, marriage, which licenses unlimited indulgence and disregards all thought of the welfare of society; John Tanner in act 4 expresses himself similarly when he declares to Malone "that mere marriage laws are not morality."

Spontaneity and flexibility are all but absent from our current formulations and our applications of them, whereas they are the qualities most essential to valid moral judgments. The codified abstraction, when it substitutes an idealization for a fact, leads to the immorality of the closed mind and the atrophied sympathies.

For one sensitive to the transcendent implications of the great abstractions, the lures which the Devil uses to tempt men from realizing to the full their best selves will seem trivial indeed. Yet the majority of men are more interested in the pleasures of the moment than in the possibility of attaining spiritual grandeur. The Devil plays on their fears by suggesting—as he does to the rebel against his authority, Don Juan—that aspiration will probably end in disillusionment and that pleasure should be pursued lest the powers of enjoyment be dulled.

In hell, as the Statue informs us, prayer is abrogated because it implies hope; if a prayer is granted, we have the responsibility of acting upon what has been given us. Dante had realized this truth, says the Statue, and had placed over the door of hell his famous injunction, "Leave every hope behind ye who enter." Don Juan excoriates hell then because it offers no hope and challenge, no opportunity for the development of conscience and responsibility. In Shaw's hell the higher purpose is always sacrificed for the gratification of the lower inclination. The will is in abeyance; hence "to be in hell is to drift."

On the contrary, "to be in heaven is to steer"; there one uses his will to achieve a vibrant existence. Heaven is "the home of the masters of reality" for, as John Gassner says, "strong minds and spirits reject second-rate gratifications." There is a "false" Heaven where weak minds and spirits pretend to like the genuine and first-rate; such was the Heaven the Statue knew before he saw the error of his ways and came to Hell. Many are in Heaven, he says, not because they are happy but because they think they owe it to themselves as "respectable" souls to be there. Since Heaven is what one most deeply desires, it will be for the respectable an eternity of uncomfortable respectability and spiritual status-seeking. For the truly regenerate, it will be an abode which encourages an infinite aspiration. The Devil's boast that "the blest" are "a continually dwindling minority" simply indicates the lack of any widespread sense in the after-life that existence to be meaningful must be dynamic. If hordes come to Hell, this indicates that the aims of men are low both on earth and in the after-life. Men would live comfortably, not dangerously.

Not so Don Juan. He places before himself a high standard of excellence, and he would agree with Faust, "Restless activity proves the man."

In the heaven to which he aspires one struggles acutely and faces reality: "You live and work instead of playing and pretending," with the result that "your steadfastness and your peril are your glory." In contact with the Life Force, as Shaw expressed it elsewhere, "courage, self-respect, dignity, and purpose are added unto us." The strength of Don Juan's aspirations reduces love, art, and conventional religion to insignificance for him; and he asserts that in the pursuit of his own pleasure, health, or advancement he has never known "happiness." Juan's reservation of his spiritual energies for a supreme purpose links him with Tanner when the latter explains to Ann Whitefield the birth in him as a boy of moral passion, an occurrence which made love, romance, and pleasure all seem secondary. Don Juan's aspiration is also to be linked with Shaw's own statement in the Epistle Dedicatory that "the true joy in life" lies in surrender to a great purpose that is not personal, in "being a force of Nature instead of a feverish, selfish little clod of ailments and grievances complaining that the world will not devote itself to making you happy." If the Devil and Mendoza are unthinking rebels and misguided idealists, Jack Tanner and Don Juan are conscientious rebels and purposive idealists.

Identification with the will of the world is an active process, but it has also its passive aspect. Juan's strenuous activity in part allows him to achieve a state unfettered by the tyranny of flesh in which he can spend his "eons" observing life, "the force that ever strives to attain greater power of contemplating itself." The implications of this definition and the one at the beginning of my next paragraph, it seems to me, answer critics who have been disturbed by the apparent emphasis on "process" which they naturally find in Shaw's philosophy of creative evolution. Value as well as progress is important to Shaw, as we see from the formulations here.

Both by active effort and passive ecstasy, the responsible individual allies himself to the powers of life, and becomes aware within himself "of Life's incessant aspiration to higher organization, wider, deeper, intenser self-consciousness, and clearer self-understanding." Our attainment of this degree of organization and control over life is not automatic; progress may ensue but it is not assured. The life energies, in fact, just barely win the battle against the forces of death and degeneration, because in the average man, despite his cupidity, sloth, and selfish aims, there is just enough life for him to respond to an inspiriting idea. The Devil is so eloquent in his condemnation of present society that Don Juan is forced to concede the facts he cites. The Devil is right in viewing the earth as a place of destruction and evil; but Don Juan takes heart from the fact that survival is possible at all. That form of "civilization" will persist, says Don Juan, which can produce the best rifle and best-fed riflemen. Don Juan grants the Devil that this in itself may be no cause for elation, but he also knows that the future can open out to spiritual immensity, even from such unpromising beginnings. So persuasive is the Devil at this point that we would incline to agree with Gassner that Don Juan wins more by poetry than by confutation of his opponent.

Don Juan's philosophy works in two directions. The operations of the Life Force, depending as they do upon the exertions of the subjective will, are irrational in essence; the increased intelligence toward which this ineffable force is directed is rational in essence. Paradoxically, rationality is supremely important and completely insignificant. Arguing from one side, Don Juan asserts that Man will "only be enslaved whilst he is weak enough to listen to reason." In the ineffectual Roebuck Ramsden, with his pantheon of Cobden, Bright, Spencer, Huxley, Martineau, and George Eliot, Shaw was undoubtedly exposing the inadequacies of nineteenth-century rationalism. While Shaw condemned the illusions which reduce many of our perceptions and values to lifeless conventions, he was aware that "illusory forms" clothe the great ideas and make them viable to humanity. Without such bold conceptions to enkindle the imagination, mankind would have nothing worthy of its spiritual allegiance. The irrational aspect of the Life Force is thus more important than the rational. Don Juan must be like the Faust whose "spirit's ferment far aspireth." Without the working within us of a mysteriously operating spirit—"the Holy Ghost" as Shaw elsewhere terms it—we would forever remain in an early stage of development without the will, impetus, and energy to attain a higher life.

The influence of woman has also been twofold. Whereas Don Juan deplores romantic love when it leads to a debilitating hedonism and a contracting of one's activity to the satisfaction of the sexual impulses, he has learned one great lesson from woman—one must be before one thinks. Shaw would have agreed with modern existential thinkers that man is ultimately a subjective entity at the mercy of the life energies rather than a thinking being. Man must reverse the Cartesian dictum and say, "I am, therefore I think." Woman, in fact, taught Juan the chief lesson of creative evolution: "I would think more; therefore I must be more." Woman may pervert the soul of man and become the main obstacle in the way of an artist-philosopher's orderly realization of the self, but she is also the primordial creative energy (the Erda-principle of The Perfect Wagnerite or the Lileth-principle of Back to Methuselah) that long ago gave birth to man as a supplemental being to help her in the perpetuation of life.

The Life Force is unpredictable in its manifestations; and it defeats man's attempts to confine its activities within closed, rationally imposed patterns. Will, spirit, imagination are too basic and too intangible ever to be brought under the complete purview of reason. Yet the Life Force which includes them works toward completer knowledge of itself and has evolved the philosopher as its primary agent in attaining these clearer perceptions. If Nature had wished only to attain beauty, order, and symmetry, she would have stopped the evolutionary processes, Don Juan insists, with the creation of the birds. In its upward course life is working toward brains, intelligence, understanding. A man needs not only to do something but to know why he does it. On the defensive about intelligence, the Statue observes that he is content to know when he is enjoying himself and does not wish to know why he is enjoying himself. He complains that, in any event, one's pleasures will not bear thinking about; and without conceding that Don Juan's ideas are true, he rather unexpectedly substantiates Don Juan's arguments against romance. In the debate in Hell, one of Shaw's characteristic techniques is this partial yielding by the opposition to Don Juan's views.

For achieving the purposes of the Life Force, there are two primary agents. On the irrational side, the mother-woman is with her sexual magnetism the incarnation of life itself. On the rational side, the philosophic man or the artist-philosopher builds up civilization with the energies that the mother-woman must expend upon gestation and family tasks. Let us consider the relationship between these two servants of the Life Force as Shaw elaborates them in *Man and Superman*.

In act 1 Jack Tanner discourses to Octavius upon the pernicious influence of woman. He ascribes her power to the fact that she is the agent of the Life Force for achieving its purposes, rather than her own happiness or some man's. Sex magnetism is an overwhelming force that disables attempts to control it altogether: "Vitality in a woman is a blind fury of creation." Statements like this cause Ervine to feel that the woman is a slave to nature as is the man she traps. While this is in part true, the woman—and finally the man—consider themselves more the servants than the slaves of the Life Force. Nevertheless, even at his most intelligent, the artist-philosopher is ineffective before biological energies though he may with some success guide their workings. It is perhaps only just, under the eye of eternity, that the man who is best suited to serve nature biologically will at last be unable to resist woman. Don Juan recounts how his rational faculties counselled him to resist the woman of the moment and to maintain his personal freedom, "And whilst I was in the act of framing my excuse to the lady, Life seized me and threw me into her arms as a sailor throws a scrap of fish into the mouth of a seabird." So much for the artist-philosopher past.

As for the artist-philosopher present, John Tanner finds he is galvanized before Ann at the end, "like a rabbit with a stoat," as Shaw once said. He confesses to Ann that "at the supreme moment the Life Force endows you with every quality," and immediately has an uncanny sense that this capitulation has also taken place somewhere in his ancestral past.

If the sex experience is trivial when trivial people use it for self-indulgent ends, it can also be transcendent. Thus Shaw rejects romantic love as an agency of creative evolution, but places much faith in sex itself when the partners to the union realize its significance for the race. The woman will be insatiable in her demands upon the man, insisting that he worship her, together with motherhood, family, and the hearth. Though man may have to submit to her to discharge his social responsibilities, he should not become subservient to her, Shaw would insist. Man, the philosopher, has his task to perform just as she has hers: he must attempt "in contemplation to discover the inner will of the world, in invention to discover the means of fulfilling that will, and in action to do that will by the so-discovered means." Nevertheless, he may with her satisfy his deepest anthropological instincts at the price of much interference in the short range with his cherished plans.

Structurally and thematically the Hell Scene is pivotal in the play, because it brings the representatives of radical intelligence and primordial energy, Jack Tanner and Ann Whitefield, closer together. It is left for Jack Tanner, Don Juan's descendant, to realize, however reluctantly, that only by submitting to woman can he aid the Life Force in producing the Superman. Don Juan calls sex "the universal creative energy" and the sexual experience "consecrated," but he resists to the end direct contact with the feminine principle, though it is possible Doña Ana may yet seek him out. At the end of the dream sequence, Don Juan leaves Hell for Heaven, the Devil and the Statue depart for the Palace of Pleasure, and Ana rushes into the void, crying, "A father for the Superman."

Whether Ana seeks Don Juan in Heaven since she can go there if she wills or whether as Woman Immortal she seeks, as Shaw once suggested, the "Eternal Father" to serve as sire for the Superman is not clear. What is clear is the metamorphosis of Doña Ana from a woman of excessive propriety at the beginning of the scene into a more relaxed individual by the middle (she can now admit the evasions which obtain in love and marriage), and, by the end of the scene, to the woman who throws all inhibition to the winds to serve, consciously and devotedly, the evolutionary endeavors of the Life Force. Though she is less conventional to begin with than Doña Ana, Ann Whitefield undergoes something of the same transformation when by the end of the play she has become aware of her part in the drama of creative evolution. She still resorts to subterfuge, but in talk with Jack she mentions the Life Force in comprehending terms whereas just previously she has referred to it scoffingly as the "life guards." Both sections of the play illustrate one of Shaw's most illuminating statements about the woman's relationship to the male in his Epistle Dedicatory: "The woman's need of him to enable her to carry on Nature's most urgent work, does not prevail against him until his resistance gathers her energy to a climax at which she dares to throw away her customary exploitations of the conventional affectionate and dutiful poses, and claim him by natural right for a purpose that far transcends their mortal personal purposes." Ann wins Jack irrevocably by referring to the cosmic destiny of which she is part, by saying that marriage will be for her not only happiness but biological insecurity, possibly death as she labors to bring forth the new generation. | He finds, then, that she shares instinctively some of his more articulately defined ideas in "The Revolutionist's Handbook" and elsewhere.

After his dream, Tanner is more resigned to capture by Ann than he was before. His resignation to his fate, though rueful, is not ill-humored; and he is now undoubtedly conscious in his deepest being of Doña Ana's cry at the end of the dream. It is significant that Ann catches up with him immediately afterwards and that he makes no further attempt to evade her. He of course protests to the end against the universal assumption that he will marry her; and he even tells her that he will not have her. Yet he is not entirely averse to his fate, for he has undoubtedly begun to realize that with a splendid biological specimen like Ann he may best be able to perform his experimental role in bringing to pass the birth of the Superman. He can no longer evade the implications of his own recommendations for racial betterment, set forth in "The Revolutionist's Handbook."

For this reason, the view of E. Strauss and others that Ann Whitefield is an acquisitive woman in the economic as well as the sexual sense is, I think, an unwarranted extension of the symbolism of the play. There is nothing to indicate that Ann is in part a symbol of modern capitalism. Tanner's marriage is not a compromise with capitalism nor are his denunciations of marriage at the play's end a denunciation of it. Tanner had already made his social and economic compromises before the idea of marriage to Ann put him in a panic. The marriage is in large part the result of the pragmatist Tanner's reluctant realization that he may be able to do more for the world as a pillar of society with subversive leanings than as a prophet crying in the wilderness.

Perhaps the battle between the sexes when the parties are the mother-woman and the artist-philosopher is best regarded from Tanner's point of view: "It is a woman's business to get married as soon as possible, and a man's to keep unmarried as long as he can." The statement explains Jack's denunciations of marriage in his final speeches, which, regarded in the context of the whole play, are less vituperative than critics like E. Strauss and William Irvine have suggested. They miss the quizzical humor, the self-derisive irony, the banter, and the inability of Jack to resist another chance to shock the susceptible. On the other hand, the serious drift of his words poignantly expresses his farewell to a life of independence, and they convey just that note of psychic martyrdom which another critic of the play, Kronenberger, misses from it.

The artist-philosopher's way of serving the Life Force may be less intensive than the mother-woman's but not less important. If woman symbolizes the life urge, the artist-philosopher symbolizes the human attempts to utilize best its energies. For it is his purpose "to shew us ourselves as we really are." As Tanner says, "he who adds a jot to such knowledge creates new mind as surely as any woman creates new man." Don Juan similarly praises the philosopher as the agent of the Life Force who increases its knowledge and power. Without his intelligence and his perceptions into the mysteries of existence, woman would give birth to children who would never achieve knowledge and power themselves. He is "nature's pilot" and prevents her and mankind from needless drifting. Thus man and woman at their best, like Ann Whitefield and Jack Tanner, serve the Life Force in conflicting ways. A rapprochement occurs between them because nature needs to make use of both feminine and masculine principles. As A. C. Ward has written in this connection, "The man's desire to create new thought is vain and barren unless it is conjoined to the woman's task of creating new thinkers." Jack as a result of his dream in Hell comes to realize that to each sex will be given its own role to perform. It is his task, in part, to overcome his reluctance to give up his immediate—and consecrated—aims as a revolutionist to help the Life Force in its long-term endeavors. As we have pointed out, the reluctance is considerable and the martyrdom is real.

In part, Jack Tanner and his counterpart Don Juan are to be associated with Shaw himself. In "How Frank Ought to Have Done It" Shaw implied that Tanner's reluctant capitulation to Ann had a personal basis in his own surrender to Charlotte Payne-Townshend. The aspects of Tanner to which Eric Bentley objects—his loquacity and effusiveness—really align him with Shaw. Tanner is only incidentally a "windbag," "an ineffectual chatterbox," "the traditional fool of comedy in highly sophisticated intellectual disguise." Prince Hamlet is none the less interesting for being discursive, and a gay philosopher is often the most persuasive. Like Shaw in real life, Jack Tanner is a witty and brilliant critic of the status quo even while he compromises with it in order to get a hearing at all for his radical ideas. If this partial identification between Shaw and Tanner is genuine, Irvine's view of Shaw's presentation of Tanner as primarily satirical is erroneous. Irvine stresses what is incidental, the parlor socialism of Tanner; and he concludes that the Roebuck Ramsdens of tomorrow are the Jack Tanners of today, without acknowledging that Tanner's ideas, quixotic as some of them are, are imbedded in more vital realities than are Ramsden's. Ussher's denigration of Tanner as an ineffective radical voice is also suspect when he says that Tanner "has never even smelt a trade-union office." Whether or not this is true, it is beside the point in view of Shaw's continued contention that Socialism in England, to be effective, must be a middle-class movement rather than a proletarian one. The fact remains that John Tanner in his relations to his society is what Shaw was primarily in relation to his—a genial revolutionary.

If Tanner is Shaw as socialist and social being, Don Juan is Shaw the man of heroic aspiration. The story "Don Giovanni Explains" helps define the difference. Don Giovanni has a "steadfast, tranquil, refined face" which looks over and beyond immediate objects into space, as if to indicate that his visionary intensity has an ineffable aspect. Nethercot's judgment here is succinct and helpful: Tanner "presents only a broken mundane image of the advanced man, whereas the latter [Don Juan] offers an other-world sublimation progressing in the direction of what may yet be." Like Shaw, Jack Tanner accepts his society until some better order can be evolved. Don Juan is, in some respects, more radical and impatient, as Shaw in his moments of disillusionment and exasperation became. Don Juan's abrupt departure from his compatriots in Hell is partly symbolic perhaps of Shaw's own disgust with the exploiters and irresponsibles of his day.

Shaw also pointed out that there were two halves to Tanner's role. In the first Tanner is the adroit comedian and scintillating critic who is in command of most situations and who disturbs if he does not profoundly affect his contemporaries. Halfway through act 2 a reversal occurs and Jack becomes a harried and hunted man, instead of the triumphant verbalist. The sense of this split in Tanner's life may have prompted Bentley to regard Ann as the vitalist and Tanner as the exponent of system, especially since in terms of dramatic action Ann takes over. The judgment, I think, oversimplifies the characters. Ann is, of course, the vitalist, but makes such incessant use of conventions for her own purposes that she can best be regarded principally as "a womanly woman" and only incidentally as the "new woman." Tanner is the exponent of system only to the extent that he compromises with his society in order to live in it. Tanner does possess "a sense of reality disabling convention"; the only realm of partial blindness with him is the sexual.

In some ways the character of Ann is more complex than that of Tanner. As we have just noted, she is both an exponent of the social conventions and a forthright violator of them when she has to be. She is never so innocent as she pretends to be, just as Doña Ana is never so virtuous as she would impress others as being. Shaw again gives the proper cue for the interpretation of one of his characters. In a letter to Iden Payne, he mentions Ann's "conventional propriety and self-possession" in the first scene of the play, "where she triumphs as the extremely well-bred and well-conducted young lady." The propriety would indicate that Ann is "a womanly woman," the self-possession that she is "a new woman." She is adroit and resourceful, when, for example, she acts the helpless feminine creature before two conflicting males. When Ramsden commands her not to look at Tanner's "The Revolutionist's Handbook" and Tanner indicates he may insist that she read it, she turns the situation by saying, "I am sure you would never purposely force me into a painful situation, Jack." She also knows when to treat Tanner with deference and solemnity as her guardian and when to undermine his authority by stressing his youth.

Her cheerful use of conventions to her own advantage, what Jack Tanner calls her hypocrisy, would indicate that she is a womanly woman using all her personal charm to encompass her ends. What Nethercot has said is true and provides the answer to those who have stressed Ann's "unpleasantness": "Thus her seductiveness, her fits of emotion and passion, her tricks, her lies and intrigues are part of the pattern which has been built up in her by a society which has refused to allow her to be a free individual in a state of free and equal citizens." Ann is self-centered and is able to concentrate all her energies upon the attaining of her present purpose, as she confesses to Octavius toward the end of the play: "The only really simple thing is to go straight for what you want and grab it."

Being so intent on her realization of the self, Ann passes beyond the Victorian woman—which she plays at being when it suits her—to become the independent woman of the modern era, the Doña Juana whom Shaw described in the Epistle Dedicatory as the most likely development of the Don Juan archetype in the modern age. In the attainment of her goals, Ann is unscrupulous—a "Lady Mephistopheles," a woman of "devilish charm"—though good-humored. The references to the devil may also indicate her conventional aspect if we think of the Devil in this play. Her predatory aspect is unmistakably indicated by the various animal images associated with her. She is a boa constrictor and a lioness with Octavius' head in her mouth and otherwise breaking everyone's back with her paw. According to Tanner, predatory woman is like a grizzly bear, a Bengal tiger, a queen bee, a spider, or a wasp, which kills the male or the prey it finally has no use for. He also regards her as the tame elephant which will capture the wild one. As a child, she had already developed something of this predatory role. She was then something of a Hedda Gabler in embryo, always waiting for Tanner to do something beautiful and heroic at last.

Ann, in fact, has the best of both worlds. Shaw brings this out amusingly in the second act when Tanner encourages her to revolt against her mother. Of course, Ann has never really been guided by maternal authority, though she has always gotten credit for observing the wishes of her parents.

What saves Ann is her realism and her humor. There is refreshing honesty and a quizzical zest in her views of the male sex when in the last act of the play she says, "There's no such thing as a willing man when you really go for him." She sizes up her situation accurately in the first place and then acts upon this knowledge. She also sees Tanner's blindness for what it is and thus she can cope with it: "I think men make more mistakes by being too clever than by being too good."

Ann also has a vigorous sense of humor and is much more genial than that other predacious woman, Violet Robinson. For one thing, she sees the situation between Tanner and herself from a long range as well as a short range perspective and savors the incongruities between them. Her sense of fun comes out when Jack calls her a boa constrictor; she thereupon puts her boa around his neck and then her arms. Most critics have fastened upon her hypocrisy and her subterfuges and have declared their cordial dislike of her. In 1909 Chesterton said there is "no truth or magnanimity in her"; and almost fifty years later in 1953 Arland Ussher declared her to be a "villainess of the family of Marquise de Merteuil." Such criticism, I think, fails to consider the vitality and exuberance which give her distinction, and Ussher's implies a preoccupation with evil that is foreign to Ann.

The fascination exerted by Mozart's *Don Giovanni* upon Shaw would argue the close affinity Shaw must have felt for the most Mozartian section of *Man and Superman*. In *Our Theatres in the Nineties*, he calls *Don Giovanni* "the greatest opera in the world," and speaks of Mozart's transforming the libretto into "a magical human drama of moods and transition of feeling," almost as if he were speaking of his own later achievement not only in *Man and Superman* but in *Heartbreak House* and *Saint Joan*. He mentions Mozart among the foremost of the artist-enchanters of the nineteenth century who made a dream land credible and bewitching, "who conjured up a region where existence touches you delicately to the very heart, and where mysterious thrilling people, secretly known to you in dreams of your childhood, enact a life in which terrors are as fascinating as delights; so that ghosts and death, agony and sin, become, like love and victory, phases of an unaccountable ecstasy." This could pass as a vivid description of Shaw's Hell Scene which was to be written a few years later.

The ideas and values developed in this imaginatively compelling region gather aesthetic weight and authority. As for the chief characters in the play, they acquire symbolic and philosophical depth when they are related to their counterparts in the Hell Scene. Granted that the other three acts of the play possess in Shaw's own words "elasticity and gaiety with social distinction," still the Hell Scene develops for the whole play a cosmic significance underlying these surface felicities. A successful comedy of manners becomes in the phrase of A. C. Ward "a Comedy of Purpose." The juxtaposition of a comedy of manners with a philosophical debate in the nether regions on elemental questions gives universal import to a social comedy. May we not also say that the wit and verve of the social comedy are reflected in the animated pace and pyrotechnical brilliance of the dialogue in Hell?

Don Juan in Hell

Louis Crompton

Despite his elaborate advertisement of *Man and Superman* as a Don Juan play, it is only in the third-act dream fantasy that Shaw enters into direct competition with the dozens of playwrights, novelists, and poets who have written of the famous lover. As we have seen [elsewhere], Tanner is a Don Juan only to the extent that he holds unorthodox views on sex. But even in the dream sequence, where Don Juan appears in his original guise as a seventeenth-century Spanish nobleman in company with other characters from his legend, Shaw's conception of Juan's personality is so much at odds with the popular tradition that one specialist has called the change "the most strange and complete transformation that any character of the stage has ever undergone," and a second has declared that he would not be surprised to learn that Shaw "thought of Don Juan after, rather than before, planning his play." It might at first seem likely, on the basis of the divergence of his Juan from the historical norm, that Shaw's researches into literature concerning the great amorist were merely superficial. Yet this does not seem by any means to have been the case. There is evidence, indeed, that he was familiar not only with the classical treatments of the tale by Tirso de Molina, Molière, Da Ponte, and Byron, but also with such lesser-known versions as the dramatic extravaganza by Dumas *père*, De Musset's poem, and the stories of Hoffmann and Mérimée, and that he consulted essays on the subject by a large number of scholars, including Manuel de la Revilla, Francisco Pí y Margall, Felipe Picatoste, Antoine de Latour, Philarète Chasles, Gustave Larroumet, and Maurice Barrès.

From *Shaw the Dramatist*. © 1969 by the University of Nebraska Press.

Nevertheless, it must be candidly admitted that Shaw's portrait of the Don is unusual enough to justify the critical bewilderment. The protagonist of Tirso's seventeenth-century religious melodrama, *El Burlador de Sevilla*, is articulate only in wooing women and issuing challenges to duels. No stage figure could be farther from a prophet-thinker. Shaw's Juan shares with him only his dignity and pride, and in the case of Tirso's hero this pride is not the intellectual pride of the critic and philosopher, but the class pride of the dashing *caballero*. Molière's Don Juan, on the other hand, is distinctly closer to Shaw's. The hero of *Le Festin de Pierre* (a play Shaw ranked above *Tartuffe* and *Le Misanthrope*) is a far more sophisticated person than Tirso's reprobate. He is clever and ready-witted in debate, skeptical in matters of faith and religion, and enough of an ironist to relish keenly his perception of the discrepancies between people's pretenses in matters of sex and their actual behavior.

Still, though he certainly takes us closer to Shaw, Molière's Juan is a sophister and not someone seriously concerned to solve the world's problems. And, compared to him, the roué Da Ponte created for Mozart's opera is a much less interesting man. Whatever Mozart's musical genius, Don Giovanni in the opera is merely a brave, resourceful scamp, whose mental energies go first of all into planning his intrigues and then into extricating himself from them. Where Tirso's amorist is a triumphant seducer who moves from conquest to conquest, Da Ponte, in adapting the story to the conventions of *opera buffa*, makes the Don a pursued and harassed husband—an essentially comic figure, more often a fugitive than a conqueror. But Shaw has carried the notion of the fugitive lover a good many steps further. As Shaw portrays him in *Man and Superman*, Don Juan, after a career as a womanizer, has fled his actual and would-be mistresses, given up love in disgust, and become an austere contemplative philosopher and social reformer. Indeed, in Shaw's allegorical dialogue he ends not as Juan the damned but, as Saint Juan, a member of the heavenly host, forced into the company of the redeemed by his own vital will and his boredom with the world's pleasures, amorous and otherwise.

But why ever did Shaw pick Don Juan as his spokesman if he was going to end, so to speak, by standing him on his head? It is perhaps not surprising that this riddle has teased literary historians, since the answer in fact lies outside literary history and in Shaw's own biography. It may seem at first wildly paradoxical that a modern revolutionary of a Puritanical bent should choose as his mask a Renaissance nobleman-rake. It is not, of course, unprecedented to find a Puritan arguing for sexual liberty; Milton and Bucer would be early examples, and the Oneida Perfectionists more recent ones.

But a Puritan Casanova is perhaps a degree more unlikely. Yet this is exactly the reputation Shaw himself earned in the eighties among his Fabian friends. His nickname in this circle, was, indeed, none other than Don Giovanni, an epithet he bore partly for his well-known enthusiasm for Mozart's opera and partly for his numerous philanderings, carried on both out of natural curiosity and with an eye to his future career as a literary psychologist. Shaw himself pointed to the paradox when he wrote candidly to a French friend, Jules Magny: "As to 'les séductions de la femme,' I believe opinion is divided between the people who regard me as a saint or a statue, and those who suspect me of being an Irish Don Juan who will eventually compromise Socialism by some outrageous scandal of the Parnell sort."

Eventually, however, Shaw came to feel that his reputation was absurdly in excess of the facts. In 1887 he even adopted an ingenious method of setting the record straight. In a fantastic short story which he entitled "Don Giovanni Explains," Shaw causes the ghost of Mozart's hero to materialize before a girl in a railway carriage and to elaborate on the situations that resulted in his being mistaken for an avid pursuer of women. The explanation is, in effect, nothing more nor less than Shaw's own apology for himself. Giovanni-Shaw admits that his friends considered him "eccentric, wanting in earnestness, and destitute of moral sense." Nevertheless, the ghost protests that he was, in fact, a man "much more highly evolved than most of my contemporaries, who were revengeful, superstitious, ferocious, gluttonous, intensely prejudiced by the traditions of their caste, brutal and incredibly foolish when affected by love, and intellectually dishonest and cowardly." After this riposte, the mock Spaniard goes on to tell how his first mistress conquered his shyness, the details of the episode being apparently those of Shaw's own real-life seduction by Mrs. Jenny Patterson:

> At last a widow lady at whose house I sometimes visited, and of whose sentiments towards me I had not the least suspicion, grew desperate at my stupidity, and one evening threw herself into my arms and confessed her passion for me. The surprise, the flattery, my inexperience, and her pretty distress, overwhelmed me. I was incapable of the brutality of repulsing her; and indeed for nearly a month I enjoyed without scruple the pleasure she gave me, and sought her company *whenever I could find nothing better to do.* It was my first consummated love affair; and though for nearly two years the lady had no reason to complain of my fidelity, I found the romantic side of our in-

tercourse, which seemed never to pall on her, tedious, unreasonable, and even forced and insincere except at rare moments, when the power of love made her beautiful, body and soul. Unfortunately, I had no sooner lost my illusions, my timidity, and my boyish curiosity about women, than I began to attract them irresistibly. [Italics added.]

After this account of his introduction to sexual intercourse, Giovanni goes on to explain that he had no designs on either Doña Ana or Zerlina, and that Elvira was simply an insanely jealous woman who (like Mrs. Patterson) first invented and then believed absurd tales about him. The Don-Juan-in-hell scene of *Man and Superman,* written more than a decade later, simply carries the cryptobiography a stage further. In it, Juan's history of his education in the arts recapitulates Shaw's career as a critic of painting, music, and drama in the London press; and both the jealous possessiveness Juan finds in his female admirers and his own clear-sightedness about his love-making closely match Shaw's own experience.

But the Don-Juan-in-hell scene is more than just covert autobiography: it is also a statement of Shaw's theology of salvation. The basis of his theology is also to be found in embryonic form in "Don Giovanni Explains." There Giovanni tells of being borne off to a hell made up of "brutish, weak, good-for-nothing people, all well intentioned," who despised heaven-dwellers as "unfeeling, uppish, precise, and frightfully dry in their conversation and amusements." *Man and Superman* develops this allegory with such paradoxical ingenuity that Shaw, finding he had left most of his readers bewildered, provided an analytical program note for the first production in 1907. In this commentary he explained that the "higher theology" rejects the hell of popular religion, holding instead that the world itself "may be made a hell by a society in a state of damnation: that is, a society so lacking in the higher orders of energy that it is given wholly to the pursuit of immediate individual pleasure, and cannot even conceive the passion of the divine will."

Shaw's hell is not the home of thieves, murderers, and ravishers, but of happiness-seekers, despairing cynics, and the self-indulgent. The hellish spirit is the spirit that fosters connoisseurship in art, dilettantism in literature, and sentimental amorism in personal relations. In a word, it is what inspires the whole round of social pleasures and organized amusements our well-to-do middle classes indulge in, from the crude vulgarity of a Las Vegas to the refinements of the Glyndebourne and San Francisco opera. Above all, it smacks of the theater. In hell as Shaw conceives it, everything is make-believe: any woman may, like an actress in make-up, be any age she likes, and any male may, like a vain actor parade with a padded figure more statuesque than any nature has provided for him. The hell-dwellers are obsessed with glamor, and with youth, beauty, and love. Those were the preoccupations of the London stage in the nineties, and they remain the preoccupations of Hollywood and television in our own day.

Shaw's devil, like the entrepreneurs of the amusement world, serves up his concoctions with an air of forced good-fellowship and touchily resents critics as carping malcontents who do not know how to enjoy themselves. Seen from this angle, he resembles both the turn-of-the-century impresario and the modern movie producer, with his facile sentiment, his cynicism, and his belief in popularity as a measure of worth. Shaw wanted him to be played by the same actor who played Mendoza, because in Shaw's London, such men were often Jews, though Shaw warns us in the preface to the *Plays for Puritans* that there is little consolation for anti-Semites in this fact, since Jewish tastes in entertainment differed from Gentile tastes only in being more romantic and markedly less coarse.

Shaw's hell is his revenge upon the English theater for the four years of ennui and disgust he suffered as a critic. In the same preface, he indicts the stage for attempting to substitute "sensuous ecstacy" for "intellectual activity and honesty." This he denounces as "the very devil." In the hell scene of *Man and Superman* Shaw gives material form to his metaphor in the shape of a devil who is before all else a hedonist. Now hedonism, of course, was far from being the avowed creed of the late-Victorian middle classes. Consequently the devil is every bit as much at odds with conventional morality as Juan-Shaw is. It is simply that their reactions to it have taken totally different directions. For Shaw's religion of struggle and reform, the devil has substituted a religion of love and beauty. He has made up his creed out of the neopagan lucubrations of men like Swinburne, Symonds, and Wilde in England and Gautier and Anatole France (in his pre-Dreyfusard days) on the Continent. To savor intensely the pleasures of art and the delights of cultivated personal relationships is the whole of his existence. What Pater stands for in a scholarly and intellectual way in his *Studies in the History of the Renaissance*, the devil represents, say, on the level of a relisher of Fitzgerald's translation of the *Rubáiyát*.

Shaw considered happiness not the aim of human existence, but a by-product of useful activity. Like Carlyle, he rejected the hedonistic calculus of pleasures on the ground that the surest way to achieve misery was to seek happiness directly. The literary hedonists of the late Victorian period were, however, for the most part avowed pessimists from the start, their creed being "Let us eat and drink, for tomorrow we shall die." Shaw looked on such men first as denizens of a post-Darwinian world for whom "the alternative to believing silly things about God seemed to be blank materialist Hedonist atheism," and second, as the latest heirs of a long and distinguished literary tradition stretching back to Ecclesiastes. The devil is thus simultaneously the spokesman for a specifically *fin de siècle* despair and the representative of a line of writers as diverse as Shakespeare, Swift, Thackeray, and Hemingway, all of whom have taken as their text "Vanity of vanities," and been overwhelmed by their sense of the futility and senselessness of the human condition. As a result, the eloquent speeches which Shaw puts into the mouth of the devil are a compliment to the literary distinction of those writers, whose majestic rhetoric and seductive poetry Shaw recognized at the same time that he deplored their will-sapping conclusions.

But how do three people as different as Juan, Doña Ana, and the Commander happen to turn up in the devil's kingdom? Here Shaw indulges his penchant for impish humor. In "Don Giovanni Explains" the Don is sent to hell in error on the recommendation of the Commander, who had mistaken him for a bon vivant on the strength of his reputation—much as if Shaw's fame as a witty scoffer and womanizer had won him an invitation to join an Omar Khayyam club. Ana's arrival in hell, on the other hand, is a satire on conventional piety. Ana, unlike Juan, has rigorously repressed her own natural inclinations and lived by the moral code of her day. She has not sacrificed her desires, however, out of any real passion for virtue, but in hopes of a substantial postmortal reward. When she wakes up in hell she complains that she could have been "so much wickeder" and that all her good deeds were "wasted," thus revealing where her real regrets lie. At first she argues that she has been sent to the wrong place, but it soon turns out that her Christianity has its own "hellish" side. Temporarily wearied by the trials and struggles of life, she had rashly assumed that the eternity of bliss promised by popular religion would be to her liking. In short, Shaw makes Ana a concrete illustration of Nietzsche's caustic remark that the orthodox Christian was a man who carried the Epicurean principle as far as it was possible to carry it.

If Ana is Everywoman in her unreflecting piety, the Commander is Montaigne's *homme moyen sensuel*. As an easygoing philistine he takes his pleasures for granted and is quite content to let the premises of his existence go uncriticized, even to the point of killing other men for doing what he has done himself, simply because he thinks society expects him to. Amiably thickheaded, he enjoys the debate between Juan and the devil as a kind of diverting sporting contest and is only shocked when Juan strips off the sentimental veils he has cast over his own sexual escapades. Unlike his daughter, whose instinctive vitality finally takes her out of the devil's realm in quest of something more than idle amusement, the Commander is one of the truly and naturally damned. His temporary sojourn in heaven is merely the consequence of a pretended interest in serious questions he had feigned for propriety's sake, which he now drops with relief, just as an ordinary man whose wife had dragged him to a community meeting might escape afterward to a bar or nightclub.

The heaven the Commander has left out of tedium Don Juan hails as the home of "the masters of reality," who work and live instead of merely pretending. If Juan's scorn of hell embodies Shaw's animus against the theater, his joy in escaping to heaven expresses the feelings with which Shaw gave up play-reviewing in 1898 to devote himself to work on the St. Pancras Borough Council. There he labored on the health, electric, housing, and drainage committees, even relishing garbage problems when he recalled his enforced theater going. "I love the reality of the Vestry and its dustcarts," he wrote happily, "after the silly visionary fashion-ridden theatre." Shaw's heaven is thus a kind of cross between a Fabian committee room and a town council session. Metaphysically, it is the sum of all true values, social, political, intellectual, and aesthetic. We learn that Rembrandt arrived there when he could draw an old woman with as much pleasure as a young girl. Mozart has also entered the transcendental regions, presumably through writing *The Magic Flute*, which Shaw regarded as a philosophical prelude to Wagner's *Ring*. As to Wagner himself, Shaw appears to accept Nietzsche's view, expressed in *The Case of Wagner* and *Nietzsche Contra Wagner*, that, having passed through an earlier triumphant phase in *Siegfried*, where he showed the world liberated by a free spirit and immoralist, Wagner then fell into decadence, going over to the devil's side by preaching not affirmation of the will, but Schopenhauerian negation in *Parsifal*. Thus heaven, in so far as it is the home of artists, belongs to those whose art is a stimulus to life, not to the practitioners of an aimless "art for art's sake."

Having brought his cast before us, and having, in the light of his new theology, established the difference between the heavenly and the hellish states, Shaw now begins the great debate between the devil and Don Juan that makes up the core of the dream episode. In form this dialogue is Lucianic-Platonic. The Lucianic element is evident in the use of legendary characters and the comic irreverence that makes it seem as if here Shaw were out to realize dramatically the "gay science" Nietzsche had called for, with its "light feet, wit, fire, grave, grand logic, stellar dancing, and wanton intellectuality." By contrast, the Platonic side appears in the dialectical structure of the dialogue and in the seriousness of the themes Shaw plays with. These are, in brief, first, the relation between creative and destructive forces in human society, and second, the function of women and sex in the universe.

The first inning is the devil's. To Juan's contention that man's mission is to help "Life in its struggle upward," the devil replies that man is not the vitalist Juan makes him, but a mortalist, in love with death. In a long and eloquent speech, parallel in many respects to the diatribe of the King of Brobdingnag in *Gulliver's Travels*, the devil argues that man finds his keenest delight, not in creation, but in funerals, sensational tragedies, and more and more horrendous wars. He is much more willing to spend money on munitions than on improving his squalid living conditions. Bloody victories excite him to enthusiasm, and the whole machinery of the political state is no more than an engine for torture and destruction under the guise of justice, duty, and patriotism. In the light of these grisly facts a man's wisest course is to withdraw from political life entirely in favor of the pursuit of private pleasure, since such an existence is at least relatively harmless.

So forceful and cogent are the devil's arguments that Shaw's interpreters have been seriously confused by them. Why, they have asked, if the devil is wrong, does he speak so many home truths, and ones that sound so much like Shavian truths at that? But this is, after all, no more than asking why Shaw does not make his devil simply a transparent sophist. The answer, of course, is that he rejects so easy a game. The devil, even a dilettante devil, must have his due. Shaw wants to show us not a man of straw, but a real tempter, that is, someone whose arguments might plausibly influence cultivated people who have some real knowledge of the world. The devil's indictment of society is therefore a cogent one, and we must pay this pessimistic cynic the compliment of acknowledging not only that his facts are irrefutable, but that his skeptical hedonism, in detaching him from the mere acceptance of the status quo, gives him the power to see behind social façades as no smugly complacent church-going optimist is likely to do.

But if skeptical hedonism can highlight the world's ills so tellingly, that is not to say that its picture of life is complete or that its answers are acceptable ones. Don Juan admits the devil's evidence but rejects his conclusion that man, socially organized, is simply a dangerous demoniac. This is both too melodramatic and at the same time too flattering an appraisal of human nature. Man's chief sin is not his tendency to violence, but his apathy and abjectness in the face of his social degradation. On the contrary, his willingness to kill is not his greatest failing, but a redeeming feature. Man the coward was willing to fight for religion in the Crusades, for freedom in the English and French Revolutions, and against slavery in the American Civil War. And if religious ideals and a hatred of tyranny and slavery have roused him to action, then even the devil's conventional retort that a generation after Lincoln the white factory worker is worse enslaved than the black field hand may soon lose its force; Juan predicts that the factory worker too will have his day as the result of a series of social revolutions against which, in the long run, not even mighty armadas will prevail. In man's sense of social solidarity and in his willingness to do God's work even in the face of bombs and bayonets, Juan-Shaw sees his ultimate salvation.

With this, Shaw's debaters now turn from arms and men to the subject of love and women. For the devil, woman exists solely as an object of romantic passion. To such a view Juan opposes neither popular moralism nor the philosophical "gynolatry" Comte had made fashionable among Victorian intellectuals. Instead he turns to contemporary biological speculations, especially those of the American sociologist Lester Ward. Against the androcentric view of evolution, which made man the primary and woman the secondary sex, Ward had argued that it was more logical to regard primitive single-sexed organisms (like the amoeba) as feminine, since they were endowed with what is usually regarded as the feminine faculty par excellence, namely, the ability to reproduce. According to this gynecocentric theory, the male is only a late innovation in the evolutionary scheme, a contrivance of the female to gain the advantages of cross-fertilization. But the male, though insignificant in relation to the female in some species, has in the case of *Homo sapiens* undergone an "efflorescence" so that he is able to dominate woman by virtue of his greater strength and mental capacity.

It is in the light of this theory that Juan now looks at love, courtship, and the "sacred" institution of marriage. The Commander, speaking as a man of the world who desires to enjoy his pleasures without thought, naïvely begs Juan to regale them with spicy anecdotes about his adventures with women. But Juan objects that the purpose of human love-making is not the personal gratification of men or women, but the eventual creation of a race that will be godlike in knowledge, in power, and in self-awareness. Scorning the sentimental haze most people throw over their love escapades, Juan proceeds to analyze his experiences with all the cold clarity of a Stendhal or a Schopenhauer. When his education in the arts made him curious about women, he began to study them at first hand, but though he was fully aware of the extent to which the real flesh and blood fell short of his ideal, the experiment soon proved fatal to his critical detachment: once he had moved into near proximity the racial urge swept him irresistibly on, propelling him into mating in spite of himself.

When the shocked Ana protests that such conduct is immoral and that men must be held to strict fidelity in their sex relations, Juan, playing the skeptical *philosophe*, retorts that, on the contrary, the life force cares nothing for chastity at all. Ana objects that marriage at least "peoples the world," but Juan, seizing the teleological point he had made earlier—that the end of marriage is the perpetuation and improvement of the species—asks if our present form of Christian monogamous marriage really does it in the most effective way. In taking this position, Shaw no doubt had in mind such convictions as Ward's that "all attempts on the part of society to regulate the relations of the sexes, necessary though they may be to the maintenance of the social order, interfere with the biologic principle of crossing strains and securing the maximum variation, development, and vigor of the stock," as well as warnings like this by Havelock Ellis:

> A cosmic conservatism does not necessarily involve a social conservatism. The wisdom of Man, working through a few centuries or in one corner of the earth, by no means necessarily corresponds to the wisdom of Nature, and may be in flat opposition to it. This is especially the case when the wisdom of Man merely means, as sometimes happens, the experience of our ancestors gained under other conditions, or merely the opinions of one class or one sex. Taking a broad view of the matter, it seems difficult to avoid the conclusion that it is safer to trust to the conservatism of Nature than to the conservatism of Man. We are not at liberty to introduce any artificial sexual barrier into social concerns.

Hence, a woman like Ana, Juan points out, might have done the race an even greater service if she had borne her twelve children not to one but to twelve different husbands.

This is Juan's reply to the conventional moralist. But what significance do these speculations on marriage have for the devil, who, after all, is not a moralist, but only a hedonist who does not want his private pleasures interfered with? The answer is, Shaw thinks, that our present-day marriage arrangements may serve the devil's purposes very well. Modern methods of birth control, by allowing cultivated people to realize the kind of love idyll hitherto confined to story books, make it possible to turn marriage partnerships into a kind of antisocial *égoïsme à deux*. In the eyes of Shaw the utopian social philosopher, a one-woman harem is a harem still, and monogamous marriage owes a good deal of its popularity to the fact that, as Tanner expresses it in "The Revolutionist's Handbook," it "combines the maximum of temptation with the maximum of opportunity."

But Juan rejects any kind of stasis, even an idyllic-erotic one:

> I tell you that as long as I can conceive something better than myself I cannot be easy unless I am striving to bring it into existence or clearing the way for it. That is the law of my life. That is the working within me of Life's incessant aspiration to higher organization, wider, deeper, intenser self-consciousness, and clearer self-understanding. It was the supremacy of this purpose that reduced love for me to the mere pleasure of a moment, art for me to the mere schooling of my faculties, religion for me to a mere excuse for laziness, since it had set up a God who looked at the world and saw that it was good, against the instinct in me that looked through my eyes at the world and saw that it could be improved.

Nevertheless, it is one thing to have such aspirations and another to assume that they correspond to anything in the permanent order of nature. The devil scoffs at Juan's faith that nature has a purpose. To adopt such a view is, to him, to follow a false analogy: it is no more logical to argue that nature must have a purpose because Juan has one than to argue on the same grounds that nature must have fingers and toes. Juan's reply is that nature's will and his are not separate, since the human will itself is simply the highest embodiment of nature's intention, and that, moreover, nature has, against all likelihood, actually turned digitless creatures into digited ones in response to some blindly felt need in man's nonhuman ancestors. Now, he declares, it is only necessary for man with his newly won intellectual powers to assume the role of nature's pilot, rather than drifting like the devil, absorbed in the sterile contemplation of love and beauty.

Juan's optimism makes the devil laugh with the disillusionment of the confirmed cynic who believes it is totally futile to seek anything from life but the delights of the passing hour. Life for him is "an infinite comedy of illusion," a series of repetitive cycles leading nowhere, the emptiest of vanities. At this point, Juan and the devil have, so to speak, fought their duel to a standstill and arrived at the rock-bottom premises of their respective faith and no-faith. Neither can finally refute the other logically. Only an act of will can resolve an impasse which has its roots in fundamental temperamental differences. Shaw, as we have seen, is theologically a Neo-Calvinist who believes that character is fate and that on this basis individuals are either predestinately damned or saved. The devil enthusiastically embraces his damnation by remaining in hell; Juan instinctively seeks his salvation by leaving it. For either to choose otherwise would be to condemn himself to an eternity of boredom, and this, the most appalling fate of all, Juan refuses to face.

Shaw even has a certain amount of respect for the devil as someone who at least does what he really wants to do and not merely what society thinks he should. By contrast, Ana may look like a naïvely duped victim of social convention. Yet in the final test we discover that she is not, like her father and the devil, among the naturally damned. Dismissing their romantic and sentimental ideals of womanhood with contempt as phantoms of the male imagination, she stoutly defends flesh-and-blood wives. Ana, Shaw tells us, is "incapable both of the devil's utter damnation and of Don Juan's complete supersensuality." She cannot, "like the male devil, use love as mere sentiment and pleasure," nor can she, "like the male saint, put love aside when it has once done its work as a developing and enlightening experience." But where her circumscribed intellect cannot save her, her womanly procreative instinct can, and it is as Woman Immortal that she pursues Don Juan to heaven, demanding, with the compelling urgency of someone who realizes that her work is not yet done, "a father for the Superman."

I have analyzed Shaw's hell scene in some detail because it has so often been treated as a mere literary *jeu d'esprit*, instead of being recognized for what it is—a classical philosophical dialogue shot through with comedy and wit and an ironic sense of human character. Whether one accepts Shaw's arguments or not will depend, of course, on one's basic attitude toward evolution, revolution, and marriage. It is not likely that Shaw will change the minds of those who think that efforts at social reform are useless, that biological change is somehow or other both a matter of pure chance and absolutely predetermined, and that our modern sentimental-domestic ideal of marriage is immutable. But anyone who is willing to think openmindedly about these matters will find himself challenged. As to the present-day relevance of Shaw's hell, aesthetic hedonism as an avowed and philosophically held creed is no longer fashionable, and, in the age of the absurdists, influences serious literature so little that its revival would be an interesting novelty. Yet, as a lived rather than a professed way of life, can anyone doubt that it is the real religion of our cultivated middle classes and especially of those university teachers who are not mere philistines? Shaw's dialogue is a profession of faith and a call to action, intended to summon us from the art gallery, the concert hall, the foreign-movie house and the cocktail party to deal with the awkward and difficult problems of the real world.

The Play of Ideas in Act 3
of *Man and Superman*

Charles A. Berst

Since Shaw wrote more in the tradition of the well-made play than he would have cared to admit, act 3 of *Man and Superman* is exceptional, being as pure a play of ideas as he was to produce. The setting, "omnipresent nothing . . . utter void," and the sense of timelessness are forerunners of expressionist theater, as are the central concerns regarding the nature of reality and man's relationship to the universe. Paradoxically, the act is both extraneous and central to the drama which surrounds it. It can be dispensed with, and usually is, on grounds that it is just too long to include in an already full-length play. More significantly, it is in some aspects a digression, operates in a different mode from the rest of the material, delays the immediate well-made story line, and much of its subject matter is already implicit in the rest of the play. The play performs well without it. However, the scene does have a greatness and power which contribute strongly to the proximate action. It works as a variation on a theme, an intellectualization, a reflection on issues pertinent to the total context, and also promotes a sense of metaphysical, archetypal, and universal dimensions which stir up, point up, and broaden the implications of the play. In one sense it elevates the action by relating it to myth and cosmology; in a further sense it chastens the action by subjecting it to a dialectic.

The most artful aspect of act 3 is that it presents a reality inverse from that of the rest of the play. On earth, reality is the social game of the "trumpery story" of acts 1, 2, and 4, and as Tanner's abstractions run at

From *Bernard Shaw and the Art of Drama.* © 1973 by the Board of Trustees of the University of Illinois. University of Illinois Press, 1973.

cross-purposes to omnipresent social assumptions he appears ridiculous and irrelevant. Social values are the *sine qua non* of life. In the hell scene, conversely, Tanner's contemplative ambitions (as represented by Don Juan) are the reality, while the social pursuits of hell are illusion. The society of earth has been consigned to hell, presumably below the stage trap and represented here by a sentimental Devil and a hedonistic Statue. Juan is triumphant over those same social attitudes which render Tanner foolish. The trumpery story is consequently given a new context which alters our appreciation of its nature and the significance of its characters. As the difference between heaven and hell is objectified by the difference between the contemplative spirit seeking self-understanding and the hedonistic spirit seeking happiness, Tanner is put on the side of the angels. He represents all that is positive and evolutionary, while society represents that which is stagnant, illusory, and self-destructive. His theories of the philosopher man versus the Life Force woman are given cosmic respectability, and the resulting inversion of fundamental assumptions as to what is real, realistic, and desirable gives the entire play a complex moral ambiguity. Ironic crosscurrents serve to cross-fertilize aesthetics and thought. The comedy of Tanner is both leavened and deepened by allowing his philosophical notions free development, while Juan's metaphysics are made immanent through being parodied in the action. As sober second thoughts underlie the comedy, a smile attends the philosophy.

This smile is the result of a triple level of cross reference, act 3 being linked to the rest of the play thematically as well as dramatically and psychologically. References in the first two acts to the diabolic, the Promethean aspect of Tanner, the Everywoman aspect of Ann, and Don Juan as Tanner's ancestor, followed by the Spanish Sierra environment and the novel band of brigands in act 3, function as dramatic steps in an increasing aura of fantasy which moves both the audience and Tanner into the dream world. The characters and ideas in hell are extensions of those in the play. There are images in common with other acts (man as bird caught in a net), character traits in common (the protagonist talks too much), and kindred speeches (in act 4, Octavius romantically repeats the Statue's words regarding love in age). Most important, the hell scene unfolds as a reasonable projection of Tanner's subconscious. He is, after all, in Don Juan's country, and the Devil as Mendoza-sentimentalist, the Statue as Ramsden-hypocrite bound for hell, Doña Ana as Ann's Life Force threat, and Don Juan as Tanner-reformer-philosopher headed for heaven are all consistent with what might well be Tanner's metaphysical and metaphorical characterizations of them. He falls asleep disapproving of Mendoza's maundering over Louisa— the man is a monomaniac, the very devil of a sentimentalist; he sees Ramsden

as a stony Statue, at last aware of reality—"Juan is a sound thinker, Ana. . . .
I was a hypocrite." His Juan is a refined, ascetic idealization of himself, and
Ana is his own naïve version of Ann—conventional, hypocritical, seeking
at last a father for the superman. There is, in addition, fine implicit comic
effect in the audacity which presumes to define the bounds of heaven and
hell, an audacity and self-confidence quite like Tanner's. The scene, thus
developed dramatically and psychologically as Tanner's, is second cousin
to Strindberg's dream plays, implicitly centered, as they are, in a single
dreaming consciousness, and developed in large part through the rambling
associations of that consciousness.

However, as a dream play or a harbinger of expressionist drama, act
3 is imperfect. The dreaming consciousness has a split personality which
operates on two markedly different levels. Most cogently the dream is
Tanner's, and serves to bind the play together in terms of his character. As
an extension of his mind, its metaphysics and mode deriving from his
preconceptions, prejudices, and forensic temperament, it offers more a tour
de force of characterization than a coherent philosophy. Consistent with
Tanner's insights, the dialectic and the myth are more immediately imaginative than ultimately convincing. The ideas are carried on streams of
Tanneresque rhetoric, and the floating abstractions, vigorously but per-
versely applied to life, are related to his role in the play. Even the ends,
bizarre, exaggerated, cosmologized, are Tanner's in substance, temper, and
spirit.

But clearly, as effective as this character development is, it is only part
of the essence of the act. Combined with it is the overriding consciousness
of Shaw. While the dreaming Tanner confers a brisk and poignant immediacy to the dream, his fundamental naïveté becomes a subject for humor.
In his exuberance his convictions approach the truth but suffer from his
unique obfuscations. Consequently, set against this intemperance is a clearer
view which serves to balance the philosophy by straightening its assumptions, perceptions, and directions. Explicitly, this authorial presence is indicated in Shaw's dramatic instinct to assign the dream also to Mendoza,
a note which does not alter the scene's intrinsic Tanneresque character but
does give the Devil's role more dialectical individuality. Implicitly, and
more important, the playwright is apparent in several key aspects—first,
in a sense of dramatic sharpness, in which the scene glows for its rhetorical
brilliance, its contentious voices, and its inversions; second, in a pervasive
sense of irony, notably removed from Tanner, irony scarcely being his
forte; finally, in a sense of an overview which gives the scene a poetic frame
of reference and binds it integrally to the play as a whole.

These two levels of consciousness serve as a subliminal complement to the vigorous dialectical voices in the scene itself. The one provides a comic link which connects the scene directly to the trumpery story, giving abstractions dramatic immediacy, while the other provides an oversoul which exploits the ironies between the drama and life, and searches more seriously for a direction between the ironies. In nearly every respect except the last, the act is a brilliant success. The extension of Tanner's consciousness in Juan, and less directly in the other hell personalities, gives the surface wit a substratum effectively founded in character. The ironic vision of the oversoul tempers all sorts of social and cosmic pomposities with a sensitive view of ignominious realities. But although this latter contributes a poetic, sardonic richness to the whole, it moves the play more toward ambiguity than resolution. Shaw's pervasive ironic-dramatic sensibility tends to undercut its own philosophic base, developing ambivalences which (similar to those in the trumpery story) make for effective art but poor philosophy. Those insights which are highly sensitive in rendering life as it is are erratic in projections regarding life as it ought to be. The playwright's wit feeds upon itself, energizing the drama at the expense of evolving a convincing thesis.

The short-range potential of this Shavian wit is impressive. Act 3, despite its elaborate intellectual content, is infused with dramatic vigor through rhetorical power, diverse characters, dialectical pyrotechnics, and an imaginative, cosmic frame of reference. Such elements transcend the stigma of so much talk and so little action, giving the ideas a dynamic context or directly vitalizing the ideas themselves. On the most obvious level, witty details sustain the vigor both of the dialectic and of the drama. These are ubiquitous, from the highly facetious to the cuttingly apt. They leap forth in brief, sharp exchanges:

> THE OLD WOMAN: Happy! here! where I am nothing! where I
> am nobody!
> DON JUAN: Not at all: you are a lady; and wherever ladies
> are is hell. . . .
> THE OLD WOMAN: My servants will be devils!
> DON JUAN: Have you ever had servants who were not devils?

They emerge in droll observations, such as the Devil's comment on Milton:

> The Englishman described me as being expelled from Heaven
> by cannons and gunpowder; and to this day every Briton believes
> that the whole of his silly story is in the Bible. What else he says
> I do not know; for it is all in a long poem which neither I nor
> anyone else ever succeeded in wading through.

Or they recur in thematic patterns, such as those which playfully and subtly effect the demolition of conventional moral attitudes:

THE OLD WOMAN: [on finding herself in hell] Oh! and I might have been so much wickeder! All my good deeds wasted! . . . Why am *I* here? I, who sacrificed all my inclinations to womanly virtue and propriety!

THE DEVIL: . . . But the English really do not seem to know when they are thoroughly miserable. An Englishman thinks he is moral when he is only uncomfortable.

DON JUAN: [Marriage is] the most licentious of human institutions: that is the secret of its popularity. . . . The confusion of marriage with morality has done more to destroy the conscience of the human race than any other single error.
. . . Nature, my dear lady, is what you call immoral. I blush for it; but I cannot help it.

More basic and effective in vitalizing thought are Shaw's inversions. By upsetting our expectations they are both dramatically startling and dialectically forceful. This he does on multifold levels. He inverts the moral significance of words and concepts—"Hell is the home of honor, duty, justice, and the rest of the seven deadly virtues"; he inverts the traditional roles of characters, turning the usual versions of Juan and the Commander topsy-turvy (as the love chase is inverted in the play); and he inverts the significance of moral and spiritual platitudes by toppling to hell most mundane notions of heaven. The result is a disorientation of conventional assumptions, the shattering of old forms to make room for new.

Finally, the cerebral level moves with dramatic vitality through vigorous shifts of thought, allusion, emotion, and rhetoric which derive from the characters' marked differences in personality and viewpoint. For example, near the beginning of the hell scene the Devil recalls Juan's singing, and he breaks into "Vivan le femmine! / Viva il buon vino!"—which the Statue takes up—"Sostegno e gloria / D'umanità," and the following dialogue ensues:

DON JUAN: . . . Hell is full of musical amateurs: music is the brandy of the damned. May not one lost soul be permitted to abstain?

THE DEVIL: You dare blaspheme against the sublimest of the
arts!

DON JUAN [*with cold disgust*]: You talk like a hysterical woman
fawning on a fiddler.

THE DEVIL: I am not angry. I merely pity you. You have no
soul; and you are unconscious of all that you lose. Now
you, Señor Commander, are a born musician. How well
you sing! Mozart would be delighted if he were still here;
but he moped and went to heaven. . . .

DON JUAN: I'll take refuge, as usual, in solitude.

THE DEVIL: Why not take refuge in Heaven? Thats the proper
place for you. [*To Ana*] Come, Señora! could you not
persuade him for his own good to try a change of air?

ANA: But can he go to Heaven if he wants to?

THE DEVIL: Whats to prevent him?

ANA: Can anybody—can *I* go to Heaven if I want to?

THE DEVIL [*rather contemptuously*]: Certainly, if your taste lies
that way.

ANA: But why doesnt everybody go to Heaven, then?

THE STATUE [*chuckling*]: *I* can tell you that, my dear. It's
because heaven is the most angelically dull place in all
creation: thats why.

The dramatic vigor, suggestiveness, and cohesiveness of this exchange reflects Shaw's aesthetic control. The implicit idea is carried by the explicit
burst of song and by the contentious discussion, with its successive emotions
of cynicism (Juan), indignation (the Devil), disgust (Juan), irritation (the
Devil), bewilderment (Ana), contemptuousness (the Devil), and amusement
(the Statue). These emotions, besides stimulating the dialectic, help to characterize the speakers—Juan, cynical, solitary, misanthropic; the Devil, romantic, hedonistic; Ana, ignorant, confused, conventional; the Statue,
spontaneous, good-humored, shallow. The nature of hell is boisterously
dramatized as *vino, femmine*, and song, and the level of intellectual development begins with Juan's reflection on this. His comment that hell is full
of musical amateurs needs but a latinate turn to read "musical amators"—
not lovers of music, but musical lovers, to whom music is intoxicating
brandy, not, presumably, an aesthetic pleasure. The Devil is consequently
twisting a bromide when he implies that his music is the sublimest of the
arts, a bromide rendered doubly invalid by the sanctity in which he cloaks
it. Juan's response to such rhetoric is withering, for obviously such talk is

hysterically banal and irrelevant to the true nature of music. And equally indiscriminate is the Devil's dilettantish comment, "You have no soul," for Juan is borne out—Mozart went to heaven, clearly not delighted by the soul music of hell. Heaven, then, is the way of the moping Mozart, who is good and appropriate company for the misanthropic Juan. The Devil remarks that heaven is a matter of taste, which has been exemplified: the taste of the sensitive spiritual temperament as opposed to the taste of the flesh-bound soul. Ana, who assumes that conventionality and popularity go together with goodness and heaven, naturally misses the point. What is conventional is not, of course, necessarily good, and wine, women, and song are manifestly more popular than heaven. The Statue, who opened this brief exchange by singing of fleshly delights, appropriately ends it as a philistine chortling over the dullness of heaven. The metaphysics have progressed from hell to heaven, the dramatic context sharply illuminating a distinct impression of both, the conceptual unit closing with a sardonic, ironic chuckle. In the process, Shaw has rapidly and poignantly effected his definition.

A paradox of Shaw's method is that in this very wit and dramatic control he ultimately compromises his argument. While the wit and drama render the cosmology vital, the philosophy seems more dramatic than sound, the beauty of the rhetorical pyrotechnics more satisfying than the logic of the discourse. Indeed, the dramatic effectiveness of the dialectic goes hand in hand with its logical difficulties. The ingenious inversions of words, characters, and concepts make for startling dialectical effects, but their artistic virtues of vitality, uniqueness, new perspectives, and sharp insights are in large part due to their violation of coherent, readily accessible associations. Major trends of thought are frequently so qualified and twisted by rhetoric that inner conviction gives way to a succession of clever points. The unsophisticated audience may well be dazzled or impressed, yet come away from the performance with a most fragmentary sense of the central meaning. Such, at least, has been the case with not a few critics.

In terms of Tanner's psychology, or in the mode of the dream play, the suprarationality of act 3 is artistically appropriate. Even the irony, which is primarily artistic and witty, as frequently challenging as confirming logic, is highly successful within its particular range. But in terms of his central argument Shaw overindulges in iconoclasm, capricious wrong-headedness, and inconsistency. By so doing he loses some of the potential for a greater art which might have arisen out of his philosophy. Thus we have Juan's doubtful proposition of eugenic breeding and, reflecting Tanner, his incomplete view of women: "To her, Man is only a means to the end of getting children and rearing them." Equally distorted is his shallow, romantically oriented view of art: "The romantic man, the Artist, with his love songs and his paintings and his poems . . . led me at last into the worship of Woman." And even more confusing is his shifting, superficial grasp of love and beauty. In one context they are physical and naïve, superior in birds over humans; in another context love is transcendent—"How do you know that it is not the greatest of all human relations? far too great to be a personal matter"; and in yet a third context both are romantic—"Here there is nothing but love and beauty. Ugh! it is like sitting for all eternity at the first act of a fashionable play." In all instances Juan is treading surfaces for the sake of making an allied dialectical point. Most obviously, he does the same sort of thing in closely proximate speeches regarding old age. He remarks, "In hell old age is not tolerated. It is too real," soon following with, "You see, Señora, the look was only an illusion. Your wrinkles lied . . . we can appear to one another at what age we choose," and later, "The humbug of death and age and change is dropped because here we are all dead and all eternal." The result is a combination of three maxims: old age is inevitable, none escape it; you are only as old as you think you are; and, age is meaningless in the context of immortality and eternity. All three are expressed by Juan as fact, whereas the first is canceled by the latter two, and fact truly lies in their ironic qualification of each other.

There is further confusion in an occasional inconsistency or misplacement of dialectical voices, and in weak, inadequate rejoinders by Juan which are left as definitive. Again, these may be excused as aberrations of the dreaming Tanner, but a dramatic and logical problem exists as the Shavian voice is an aesthetic factor. An early speech by the Statue, which includes, "For what is hope? A form of moral responsibility," sounds like Juan in both subject matter and rhetorical style. On similar grounds the Devil reflects Juan when he mentions "Justice, duty, patriotism, and all the other isms," and when he concludes, regarding the superman: "The 20th century will run after this newest of the old crazes, when it gets tired of the world, the flesh, and your humble servant." Juan is guilty of gross oversimplification in his response to the Devil's strong argument regarding the power of death over life on earth. He merely asserts that man overvalues himself as bold and bad, while in reality man is only a coward. And when the Devil remarks, "You think, because you have a purpose, Nature must have one. You might as well expect it to have fingers and toes because you have them," Juan's response is woefully inadequate: "But I should not have them if they served no purpose." Further, when the Devil predicts that Juan, like all reformers, will experience "vain regrets for that worst and silliest of wastes and sacrifices, the waste and sacrifice of the power of enjoyment: in a word, the punishment of the fool who pursues the better before he has secured the good," Juan answers this penetrating, fundamental argument with a mere "But at least I shall not be bored." In sum, the dialectical dice are loaded, and while Shaw delights in strong antitheses, he sometimes dodges their implications. Had he maintained the act as a pure dream, its imbalances might have merely added to Tanner's character, but as it assumes greater pretensions, its lapses become flaws. Like Milton, Shaw is not really on the Devil's side, but his arguments against the Devil occasionally lack both balance and substance.

If we are sensitive to these lapses, we are perhaps less surprised by the greatest paradox of Shaw's entire Life Force philosophy—its fundamental conservatism. In expanding biological impulse into the Life Force, in interpreting the prophets as imperfect supermen, and in transmuting Jehovah into God in the Becoming, Shaw may convince the unwary that *Man and Superman* is "a revelation of the modern religion of evolution," but such a tag obscures the fact that this religion is as much a new dress as a new faith—more daring and contemporary than the old, but only thinly covering many attitudes basic to conventional Christian thought. Shaw is definitely not Christian in a doctrinal sense; his cosmology does not fit the slots of orthodox theology. But while his absolutes are not traditional, they have many aspects which are, and most of the moral implications he derives from them are decidedly Christian. Shaw's skeptical and rebellious stance has the virtue of subjecting old forms to irreverent scrutiny and a modern viewpoint, but finally it produces less an assertion of that which is truly revolutionary than an affirmation of old spiritual values, values revitalized and reemphasized by being shaken.

One key to the nature of a particular religion may be found in those souls it finds worthy of its heaven. In his heaven Shaw quaintly deposits that dwindling minority, "the saints, the fathers, the elect of long ago." These are the realists of Shaw's cosmos, for, as Juan remarks, "Heaven is the home of the masters of reality." Similarly, Shaw's moral base is remarkably old-fashioned. His story represents not a linear evolution from Tirso de Molina's *El Burlador de Sevilla*, as he claims in the play's introductory epistle; rather, it has many of the same morality play convictions and is preponderantly the last stage of a circular evolution. The central character may indeed appear quite different in the evolving versions: Tirso's rake of one thousand and three conquests was transmuted by the Romantic Age into a rebellious, freedom-seeking hero, and perverted by Shaw into a moralist and philosopher; the impetuosity and sensualism of Tirso's Juan are a far cry from the deliberateness and asceticism of Shaw's. But the moral theses of the two playwrights have much in common, both asserting that a life of sensuality, thoughtlessness, and irresponsibility will end in physical and spiritual destruction. Shaw has, most simply, merely switched the moral position of Tirso's Juan and the Commander—Juan is the moralist, as was Tirso's Commander; the Commander is the hedonist, as was Tirso's Juan. Shaw's Juan, from the vantage point of the hereafter, is more self-conscious and subtle than Tirso's Commander; his sense of social hypocrisy is keener, and he does not quite think in terms of sin and damnation, but the spiritual role of the two characters is similar. They are both on the side of God, and since Tirso is on the side of the Commander, and Shaw is on the side of Juan, the moral implications of the legend have come almost full circle.

This hint of Shaw's conservatism opens medieval doors. As both he and Tirso oppose the epicurean, the self-indulgent, and the physical to the ascetic, the altruistic, and the spiritual, they are in a traditional vein. Shaw even more clearly than Tirso pursues the medieval Christian dichotomies of flesh and spirit, *cupiditas* and *caritas*, reality and illusion, heaven and hell. He differs from the tradition, as we have noted, largely in his modernization of certain absolutes. For God he substitutes "Life," for Divine Providence he substitutes "Life Force." God as Life is evolving, seeking brains, self-consciousness, self-understanding. Divinity is thus more immanent than transcendent, and individual commitment to spiritual principles is more earth-oriented than in conventional doctrine, though one's mode of action should be motivated by the highest spirit. A by-product of spiritual self-consciousness is clear social vision, a vision cutting through the shallowness of ideals which rest on rhetorical symbols. In Tirso's play society offers moral direction, steering under implicit authority from God, while in Shaw only the vital and spiritual individual can steer, society being lost in moral aimlessness, drifting on its own foolish illusions.

Generally Shaw's modernism serves to stir up old spiritual distinctions. "Life" as Shaw's metaphor for God is in a long tradition of poetic and mystic attempts to delineate or symbolize the Absolute, and while Shaw allows deity considerable imperfection, treating it as a vital force in the process of evolution, his view of this force's ultimate, all-informing, ethereal nature verges on medieval mystic sensibility. Similarly, as Shaw's Life Force objectifies Divine Providence, it elicits the same Christian paradox: true free will is experienced in submitting oneself to the Life Force, as to the will of God. The man who rushes off on a tangent of his own under the guise of free will suffers extinction through irrelevance, as the sinner of

Christianity suffers extinction through countering the reality of God. Shaw gives this observation dramatic dimension through revealing that only in the role of Don Juan, in contemplative consciousness, can Tanner find true freedom as a spirit rising above society's thoughtless symbols and generalizations, a spirit presumably in accord with the Life Force and consequently free. Finally, Shaw's social distinctions, through being more sophisticated than those of Tirso's play, are actually more sensitively orthodox. Personal, social, and spiritual hypocrisy, all so frequently engendered by social pressures and aspirations, cloak subtle strains of *cupiditas*—a sure route to damnation, whether in Shaw or in Christianity.

With the talents of a modern playwright and the convictions of a socialist, then, Shaw blends morality play devices and the sensibility of a religious tradition. As he observes in his preface to *Saint Joan*, his dramatic technique and outlook are medieval when compared with Shakespeare's, and his comment in the epistle that his conscience is the genuine pulpit article is frankly set in a context of religious commitment which informs (or transforms) his socialism. Thus Shaw's Devil, who diverts men from their real purpose into drifters, resembles the Tempter of Mankind in the morality plays, and the Devil's comment that "I cannot keep these Life Worshippers" gains antiquarian poignancy in sounding like a morality play Satan foiled by the faithful of God. Conceptually, the Bergsonian metaphor of Tanner as intellect and Ann as instinct synthesizing in intuition is matched hauntingly by the suggestion of a more cosmic metaphor of the spiritual Father joining with the immortalized Mother to produce the incarnate Son. Shaw affirms this grander analogue in commenting on Ana: "For though by her death she is done with the bearing of men to mortal fathers, she may yet, as Woman Immortal, bear the Superman to the Eternal Father."

The hope which resides in this ultimate analogue is tentative, and its power depends in large part upon faith, whether one be Christian or Shavian. For Shaw has many of the same difficulties in defining his God as had the Middle Ages. Appropriately Juan comments, "Heaven cannot be described by metaphor." How can one make infinite spirit and ultimate ends intelligible to finite imagination? How is the playwright to render them dramatically, and how is the philosopher to make them comprehensible? Shaw starts by shaking the platitudes which a mundane society creates, in its poverty of language and thought, to express its ill-defined ideals. Thus joy, love, happiness, and beauty are espoused by the Devil, and thus Juan speaks of hell as "the home of honor, duty, justice, and the rest of the seven deadly virtues." The point is, as Juan observes later, that beauty, purity, respectability, religion, and so forth "are nothing but words which

I or anybody else can turn inside out like a glove." And this is precisely what Shaw does, to destroy the sacredness of these false gods. To properly assess reality, or to approach God, one must distinguish between the symbol and the fact. Shaw's psychic inversion of the roles of Juan and the Commander is a forceful, dramatic extension of this observation. But once the point is acknowledged and we are refreshed by a freedom from the tyranny of symbols, where are we? Our minds may have been cleared of cant, but surely this is only the first step toward a higher consciousness. At this juncture we may object that earlier Juan remarked regarding heaven, "You live and work instead of playing and pretending"—an assertion which rings with a good sound, but which, according to Shaw's own iconoclasm, may be questioned. Are living and working any more meaningful or sacrosanct than love and beauty? May they not just as easily be turned inside out by a relentless nihilist? Similarly, Juan speaks of the realities learned from toil and poverty, but he does not define these realities, and we suspect that were they defined they would likely be idiosyncratic to Shaw's social views. The assumption that toil and poverty are somehow a key is one which confines reality more than defining it. Clearly, once Shaw enters topsy-turvydom, all abstractions are subject to the game, and Juan's arguments are self-defeating in a world of infinite convolutions and relativities. His convictions, the foundation of his dialectic, ultimately become a faith in the transcendence of some qualities over others, and, like all faiths, his can be granted only a degree of possible truth, being confined by the limitations and aberrations of his consciousness.

Juan's faith, quite predictably, seems to emerge as a blend of metaphysics and socialism, the vagueness of the first compromised by and compromising a melodrama of the second. His sense of reality leads to notions of social revolution and then transcends social goals as it transcends humanity into a mysterious land of spiritual perfection. The suprarational (or irrational, in a pejorative sense) thrust of Juan's argument is expressed in his remark that man "can only be enslaved whilst he is spiritually weak enough to listen to reason." Intellectually, with symbols inverted and reason subverted, the dialectic moves toward chaos. While Juan denies being a spiritual hypochondriac, we suspect that to some extent Shaw is one. Thus Shaw falters, and his metaphysical ends become even vaguer than those of conventional Christianity. He has undoubtedly overreached himself, and we may realize parenthetically that Christian symbols have more value as hooks on which we can hang our imagination than danger as snares which snag us. The problem, of course, is less in the symbols than in our use of them.

In sum, Juan speaks of contemplating reality while Shaw renders his reality relative. Since in practice Shaw ultimately sacrifices logic for intuition, it seems ironic that he typifies heaven as primarily mental. Shaw's hell is easy to comprehend: it is the world, with its vanities, hypocrisies, and illusions. As Juan says, "Hell is a city much like Seville." But his heaven, deprived of hell's symbols, is incomprehensible, and Juan's denial of the flesh for the Greater Glory sounds much like Christianity's divine excuse for inhumanity: there'll be pie in the sky by and by. In abnegating flesh and the world, Juan abnegates the most immediate realities of life, delimiting his character to its cerebral essence in which spirituality is no more than vaguely implicit. As such, he is but a fragment, and the play requires living correlatives in Tanner to gain dramatic fullness and credibility. And Juan's ill-defined absolute is but an extension of his own spiritual austerity, etherealized out of human relevance. Is this the goal toward which man must steer? The Ancients in the last part of *Back to Methuselah* objectify the cerebral sterility of Shaw's conceptualization.

Compensating for the weakness of details in Shaw's argument and for the vagueness of his ends are the scope of his artistic conception and the vigor of its execution. Shaw's drama and spiritual quest are energized more by the power of iconoclastic probing and the creation of imaginative new contexts than by fully consistent or fully developed ideas. Shaw the vitalist may be caught in the dramatic impetus of his dialectic, and vitality may at times become more important than logic, but as his basic contribution involves a revitalization process, such means are inextricably bound to his ends. Thus he plugs his own genius and the twentieth century into the old metaphors of Christianity, charging act 3 with a mental energy which complements the dramatic energies of the trumpery story. The roll of the rhetoric, the inventiveness of the dialectic, and the keenness of the wit are no doubt more impressive than sound, but here these qualities have a special poetry which reaches through philosophy to music and delight. A deeper didacticism is perhaps served as intellect is orchestrated, with its movements producing an aesthetic experience in and of themselves. Most important, by presenting a reality inverse from that of the rest of the play, act 3 provides a rich cross-reference between philosophy and life, abstraction and fact, *caritas* and *cupiditas*. As it is a dramatic, psychological, and metaphysical extension of the rest, it elevates the total play on multifold levels while unifying it with a broad frame of reference. Thus despite (and partly because of) its imperfect philosophy, *Man and Superman* evolves as fine art.

Man and Superman

Maurice Valency

The first part of Shaw's career as a dramatist was a period of unbelievably
intense activity. In the course of six years, in the intervals between his many
chores—his journalistic duties, his work at the Fabian office, his research
at the British Museum, his meetings and conferences with socialist col-
leagues, the workingmen's lectures to which he devoted his spare evenings,
and the staggering load of correspondence he carried—he had somehow
managed to write ten plays, jotted down piecemeal in shorthand in pocket
notebooks, mostly while he was riding on trains and buses on the way to
some engagement.

His labors brought him virtually to the edge of death. In 1901 nothing
came from his pen but *The Admirable Bashville*, a dramatization of *Cashel
Byron's Profession*. This play, written in blank verse of the utmost banality,
was intended chiefly to preserve the stage copyright of the novel and has
since served no useful purpose. But in 1903 Shaw finished *Man and Superman*
and with this he entered upon his greatness.

In England the 1890s were a time of unusual spiritual fervor, evidenced,
on the one hand, by a powerful renewal of Christian faith and, on the other,
by a significant reawakening of interest in mysticism, magic, astrology,
and the occult. This revival of arcanic lore was strongly influenced by the
Paris school of mages, the groups associated with Sâr Péladan and Eliphas
Lévi. Essentially these movements, intimately related to the ascendancy of
symbolism in literature and the arts, were the result of a widespread reaction

From *The Cart and the Trumpet*. © 1973 by Maurice Valency. Oxford University
Press, 1973.

against the positivistic tendencies of the earlier part of the century. In France, the reaction was in some measure signalized by the enthusiastic reception of Paul Bourget's *Le Disciple*, but there is no doubt that the antecedent wave of materialism had generated its counterwave some time before Bourget made it official in 1889.

It is to this movement toward a revitalization of spiritual values that *Man and Superman* must be referred. Even before the composition of *The Devil's Disciple*, possibly as early as *The Philanderer*, Shaw had been working toward the formulation of a general idea of religious nature, something which would arrange his metaphysical notions in a meaningful pattern. In *Man and Superman* the design was for the first time unfolded in all its complexity, exemplified by a dramatic action, explained in a lengthy preface, symbolically extended through the philosophic dialogue interpolated in the third act, and supported by an appendix and a glossary of maxims in the style of La Rochefoucauld. Whatever may be thought of this performance as philosophy, it is certainly a very complete exposition of a dramatic idea, the most ambitious that anyone had so far put forth in the theater.

The action of *Man and Superman* is frankly exemplary. It involves a love story played in comic style, with episodes of melodramatic extravagance and a more or less conventional conclusion. The heart of the play is the dream sequence, a lens through which the love story is magnified to cosmic proportions, so that the characters are exhibited *sub specie aeternitatis*, or somewhere near it. The method marks a decisive change in Shaw's approach to comedy. With this play he departed from the type of realism he had learned from Ibsen, Becque, and Brieux. In *Candida* he had experimented with symbolism. *Man and Superman* was a full-scale example of symbolist drama.

By 1903 symbolism had undergone a full development on the Continent, and its influence in England was already strong. Maeterlinck had furnished the new movement with a striking manifesto, but symbolism had deeper roots than Maeterlinck imagined. The consequence of the movement against realistic representation became apparent first in literature and painting, then in music and the decorative arts. In the theater the strictly mimetic approach to drama that the naturalists professed in the name of "science" evoked a decided reaction. Plays of the type of Villier's *Axël* and Maeterlinck's *La Princesse Maleine* had given early symbolism a medieval coloring which blended readily with English Pre-Raphaelitism; but *L'Intruse* and *Intérieur* indicated other paths to the Maeterlinckian *au-delà*, and, soon after Ibsen, writers such as Hauptmann and Hofmannsthal showed what could be done to reveal the psychic landscape that the naturalistic viewpoint obscured. By the end of the century every major dramatist on the Continent was a symbolist.

It was to be some time before anyone in England showed an interest in symbolism, but before the end of the century Yeats, Synge, and later Barrie began experimenting with the new techniques. Meanwhile, in Sweden, Strindberg was developing the methods of French symbolism into what came, some decades later, to be called expressionism. *To Damascus I* (1898) and *The Dream Play* (1902) clearly indicate the course of symbolist drama in the twentieth century: with these plays Strindberg laid the foundation of what is modern in the modern theater.

Shaw had seen several examples of symbolist drama when Lugné-Poë's Théâtre de l'Oeuvre came to London in March 1895, but he does not seem to have been aware at the time of the importance of the new movement. By this time both Walkley and Yeats were deeply concerned with symbolist ideas. Shaw, however, seems to have thought of this movement as an aspect of Pre-Raphaelitism unworthy of any special attention. In the lengthy preface with which he introduced *Man and Superman* he gave no evidence of being aware of the fact that with this play he was breaking new ground in English drama.

Symbolist drama was designed to afford an intimation of the spiritual reality which lies, presumably, beyond sensual experience. To become aware of this plane of being is to perceive the significant pattern, the Idea, which orders the seeming chaos of the material world. In this connection the nineteenth-century symbolists were greatly impressed by the theory of signatures and correspondences in which the symbolists of the seventeenth century had seen a secure basis for poetry. They did not, for a time, relish Blake or Donne but they read Swedenborg avidly and, in connection with Swedenborg, Poe.

The theory that underlay their art depended, of course, on the assumption that beyond the visible world there is in fact a suprasensual reality of which the artist becomes aware when he is properly sensitized, and the nature of which he is able to suggest through a special vocabulary of symbols, that is to say, through images of unusual potency. For Swedenborg this reality was none other than the cosmic structure long ago described by Philo Judaeus and Dionysius the Areopagite, defined by Thomas Aquinas, and realized poetically by Dante.

Swedenborg was a scientist who in his later life saw visions. The symbolists who were influenced by him, however, were poets. For them, the Beyond was less clear and less rational than it seemed to Swedenborg.

It had a Platonic look; but there was no agreement whatever as to its nature, or the nature of the Idea at its core, and their visionary experiences were notably mysterious. In later times when the artist peered into the depths of his soul he was likely to find there, like Rilke, chiefly himself. The narcissistic nature of these psychic adventures led quite naturally to the probing of the unconscious by way of dream and myth; but a quest that turned in this manner upon itself left something to be desired. The symbolists had embarked on a mystic errand, much like the knights in search of the Sangreal. Their failure to find anything substantial to symbolize drove some into the church and others to despair, but their efforts nevertheless resulted in a body of exceedingly interesting literature and art.

Shaw was doubtless attracted briefly by the mystical aura of French symbolism, and he gave voice to this variety of religious experience through Father Keegan in *John Bull's Other Island*; but evidently he distrusted this poetic strain and ultimately rejected it in favor of a more energetic faith, the basis of which he found in the writings of Samuel Butler. It was through this heady blend of science and religion that ultimately he found his true vocation as a writer.

In the 1890s a sense of vocation was indispensable to a writer of serious leanings, and particularly to one who fancied himself a poet. Shelley had fixed the type of latter-day apostle in the popular imagination, and many a romantic young man believed himself to be marked, like the unknown poet in *Adonais*, with the sign of Cain or Christ. The problem of *l'homme engagé* had concerned Ibsen deeply. It was debated in his plays from *Brand* to *When We Dead Awaken*. In the circumstances a writer like Shaw could hardly avoid the need for a reliable cause to serve. In the absence of God, however, it was not easy to find an idea capable of sustaining a lifetime of dedication. There was, of course, the cause of humanity which Shaw had early adopted, but the concept of humanity was vague, and at best provisional. It was in his search for God that Shaw at last came upon the Life Force, which henceforth monopolized his efforts.

The workings of the unconscious will, which Schopenhauer had so dramatically described in *Die Welt als Wille und Vorstellung* (1818), furnished a basis considerably more interesting from a philosophic viewpoint than the vague imagery of the symbolists or the stark materialism of Marx.

Schopenhauer began to be read extensively in England only after the middle of the nineteenth century. In April 1853 John Oxenford published an account of Schopenhauer's philosophy in the *Westminster Review* under the title "Iconoclasm in German Philosophy," but it was only in 1883 that *The World as Will and Idea* became available in English. The idea that the will and the passions determine the life of the intellect was intolerable to those who insisted on the traditional primacy of the reason; but it found favor with many who disliked the bureaucratic disposition of the Platonic soul, as well as with those who were frightened by the specter of materialism, to which the rationalistic theories of the time infallibly led. The utilitarian notion that prudence is the essence of morality was particularly offensive to those who looked to a higher principle with which to justify the social concept. Schopenhauer's Will, though blind and aimless, had romantic glamor, and a spiritual quality which the dry rationalism of the positivists obviously lacked.

In spite of the fact that Coleridge and, after him, Carlyle, were strongly influenced by German ideas, German metaphysics played no great part in shaping English thought in the first half of the nineteenth century. Toward the beginning of the century there had been in Germany a growing reaction against Kantian rationalism, the result of which was a gradual shift in emphasis within the classic framework of German idealism. For Kant, as for Plato, the intellect was the primal reality. Fichte and Schelling, however, deeply influenced by such writers as Cabanis and Helvetius, saw the vital principle of reason as something immanent in the will and therefore looked to the individual, rather than to some external essence, for the sources and formative principles of belief. Such attempts to reach back of the intellect in the quest for an ultimate reality culminated in Schopenhauer's formulation of being in terms of Will and Idea.

Schopenhauer argued that reason could do no more than to arrange and classify the data of sensual perception. Science dealt only with phenomena; but behind the material world apprehended by the senses, it was possible to intuit the existence of an urge which was neither rational nor intelligible and which defied explanation. This was life itself, the vital principle. Schopenhauer called this urge the will to live. The resulting metaphysics seemed—in contrast to the idealism of his contemporaries— realistic. Its consequence in the latter part of the century was a mounting attack against rationalism and the supremacy of the scientific method which had so far dominated nineteenth-century thought. One aspect of this reaction was the symbolist movement.

It is unlikely that Shaw came directly to a knowledge of Schopenhauer's system, and even less likely that he thoroughly understood its implications, but the theory of love in *Man and Superman* seems to rest quite firmly on a Schopenhauerian basis, and it is evident that Shaw's thinking at the time of its composition was influenced by ideas that could have had no other source. For Schopenhauer the principle of life is an irrational and motiveless energy which in time develops consciousness. This is the underlying reality in which we find our kinship with whatever lives that is not man. Ideas have no creative function. Reality is revealed to us in our sense of the Will immanent in ourselves. Life is both painful and senseless. One may find palliatives, but while there is consciousness there is no escape from pain.

Schopenhauer's pessimism suited Strindberg very well, and after *Master Olaf* it furnished the groundwork of his drama until he turned in his later life once again to God. It was wholly unsuited to Shaw's temperament. What appears in Schopenhauer's system as the driving, senseless, and motiveless will is in Shaw's view motivated, sensible, and sacred. It is God, effectively dynamic in every living being, a soul of infinite potentiality striving for fulfillment through its creatures.

What the ultimate goal of its endeavor might be, aside from the attainment of perfection, Shaw was not able to imagine. It was only in *Back to Methuselah* that he attempted to come to grips with the ultimate; and the conclusion there is indeterminate. Nevertheless it is arguable that the goal of the spiritual effort which Lilith exemplifies is, in Hegelian terms, freedom, that is to say, freedom of the will. This is seemingly attainable through the development of mind. In *Man and Superman* the blessed are engaged in an apparently endless intellectual effort. Conceivably the aim of this process is the liberation of the spirit from its material entanglements to the point where it is self-conditioned and self-determined. That is certainly the direction indicated for the human adventure in *Back to Methuselah*. Shaw's idea thus appears to approximate Hegel's assumption much more closely than Schopenhauer's. For Schopenhauer the evolution of the will to live ends in extinction; for Shaw it ends in omnipotence.

Shaw doubtless passed through a period of godless materialism, but his mother was a spiritist, and he himself was in considerable need of God. By his early thirties he had read Bunyan, Blake, Butler, and Bradley, as well as other writers in the B volumes of the British Museum catalogue; doubtless he had read Schopenhauer in translation and some account of Hegel's system. In these writings he found both a basis for faith and a way to establish himself personally in the Messianic tradition. In 1889 he wrote his fellow Fabian Hubert Bland of the price one has to pay in material prosperity in order to arrive at a consciousness of one's spiritual self "as a vessel of the Zeitgeist or Will or whatever it may be." "You and I," he concluded,

> have followed our original impulse, and our reward is that we
> have been conscious of its existence and can rejoice therein. The

coming into clearer light of this consciousness has not occurred to me as a crisis. It has been gradual. I do not proceed by crises. . . . My tendency is rather to overlook change in myself, and proceed on absolute assumptions until the consequences pull me up with a short turn.

Shaw was at that time thirty-three, and well on the way to something like a definition of his "spiritual self." He had reviewed Butler's *Luck or Cunning?* two years before for the *Pall Mall Gazette*, in 1887, without giving any indication that it held any special meaning for him. But its influence on his thinking was evidently immense. Twenty years later he was so sure of his metaphysical position as to declare with pride that he was "implacably anti-rationalist and anti-materialist."

In reaching this position Shaw followed the major trend of the time. In the 1880s materialism was no longer in vogue. Comte had long ago come to the conclusion that, since in the nature of things the search for final causes was fruitless, society could do no better than to abandon the quest for ultimate truth in order to seek out such knowledge as might be immediately useful. From this viewpoint the philosophical method of the future would necessarily be empirical rather than speculative, and the systematic establishment of data would constitute a necessary prerequisite to any formulation of the laws that govern human relations. It was Comte's intention to emancipate his age in this manner from the tyranny of religion. Instead he condemned it to the despotism of science. In France the positivists, after having, with considerable fanfare, abandoned the search for the ultimate, proceeded to advance improbable generalizations ostensibly derived through scientific procedures. The result was a form of authoritarian dogmatism more arbitrary, less credible, and much less agreeable than that of the church.

In England, Mill had already attempted in a similar fashion to apply empirical methods to social phenomena, but, as he was the first to admit, without success. Though supernaturalism had been by this time effectively banished from the laboratory, it continued to haunt the minds of all but the most confirmed rationalists. In the case of Mill it was evident that his approach to philosophy was seriously hampered by his unwillingness to accept a rigorous determinism. In an age that had reluctantly accepted Darwin without quite giving up God, the need to affirm the free will of man was felt to be of critical importance, and the ability of humanity to perfect itself through its own efforts seemed especially demonstrable. Thus Mill's essay *On Liberty*, published in 1859, was vastly more influential than

any of his more closely reasoned theses; and his faith in the essential goodness of man, the infallibility of reason, and the fundamental morality of
mankind had—as his last essays indicate—more religion in it than logic.
Even John Morley, a most determined agnostic, found it impossible to give
up his quite unscientific belief in the sanctity of human nature, although
he was unable to see Comte's deification of humanity as other than an
empty metaphor.

The school of idealistic thought that was associated with Oxford in
this period, together with the influence of such anti-positivist works as W.
H. Mallock's *The New Paul and Virginia* (1878) and *Is Life Worth Living?*
(1879), opened the way for a developing anti-intellectualism of respectable
proportions, and in England many were impelled to look beyond logic for
an acceptable spiritual principle. For a socialist of Shaw's temper it was no
great feat to discover somewhere in the vicinity of the Schopenhauerian
Will and the Hegelian *Weltgeist* a congenial principle of divinity. In spite of
the absence of any demonstrable basis for such an assumption, the idea of
an evolving spirit immanent in its creatures, blind to begin with, but ultimately all-seeing, seemed to him to afford a ready avenue to a believable
religion.

In 1881 Frederic Harrison, the most articulate and most prolific of the
English positivists, instituted the Positivist Church in London at Newton
Hall in Fetter Lane. It was in this church that Cyril Sykes's parents are said
to have been wed in Shaw's *Getting Married*. This notable experiment in
adult education was organized around a library selected by Comte himself.
It was intended to develop the idea of "man's dependence on the human
Providence which surrounds him from the cradle to the grave." Harrison's
position was staunchly positivistic, but he was deeply concerned also with
the search for a general idea, a synthesis which might serve as a rational
basis of faith. As the religious views which Harrison sought to develop
involved the worship of humanity as the *grand être* of Comte, it reconciled
a strictly rationalistic idea of the human enterprise with a mystical out-
pouring of veneration for the vital principle at its core. It was this kind of
thinking that Shaw had in mind in speaking of the "new theology."

In the 1860s Schopenhauer's work was tolerably well-known in England, but it took some years more for the Victorians to become aware of
Hegel. In 1865 J. M. Stirling published *The Secret of Hegel*, a valiant attempt
to interpret *The Phenomenology of the Spirit* (1807). Soon thereafter an influential school of English writers headed by F. M. Bradley and T. H.
Green heralded a strong idealistic reaction against Millite rationalism and
the vestiges of Bentham. Mill, like the humanists of an earlier age, had

concluded that pleasure is the highest good, but in his view the individual's pleasure lay in the pleasure of others. This charitable concept, which Mill himself eventually abandoned, Bradley scorned as a utilitarian remnant and in his *Ethical Studies* in 1876 he asserted the view that pleasure, in the utilitarian sense, was an empty abstraction. To Bradley it seemed that the only reality was the life of the mind, and that the goal of evolution was the Absolute, the highest determination achievable by a self-creating and self-subsistent God. With this Absolute the intermediate human self in its truest reality could be identified through faith and, in this manner, man might attain to an immediate intuition of God. Faith meant, in Bradley's judgment, both the belief in the reality of an object and the will that this object be real. Thus the active principle in evolution was neither intellect nor desire, but will in its creative aspect. The implication was that mind is a self-creating entity in continuous development.

Bradley's system departed in some ways from the usual interpretations of Hegel, but essentially they reached the same conclusions. The Hegelian dialectic is a spiritual process in which, taking account of the contradiction inherent in every finite statement, the intellect strives to overcome this contradiction by an appropriate synthesis on a higher level of understanding. Knowledge thus unfolds through the inner stress of its own contradictions, proceeding from the simplest formulations through progressively more complex stages of comprehension until it reaches its fulfillment in the Absolute. The development of the human spirit is thus seen to be the progressive revelation of God, whose reality as intelligence is manifested in the human self-consciousness alone as it develops into complete and perfect self-awareness.

It is obviously more sensible to relate Shaw's conception of the Life Force to the English idealists of the 1870s—the more so as Bradley wrote a brilliant style—than directly to Hegel's *Geist* or to the *élan vital* which Bergson described in *L'Evolution créatrice* of 1907. Without doubt, Shaw's ideas differ a great deal from Bradley's in ways that are of significance to specialists, and even more from Hegel's, but to the unaided eye they might seem remarkably similar. Shaw was certainly no philosopher, though he struck philosophical poses, and still less a scientist, though he liked to think of himself as one, but he was well abreast of the principal thought of his time. The idea of an aspiring element at the heart of being was widespread in the speculative fancies of an age that was deeply infected with evolutionary concepts. Motion and change were indispensable factors in the etiological patterns of the time, as indeed they are now, and Bergson's substitution of durational values for the fixed forms of classical philosophy came at a moment when it could shock nobody. Hegel's system had special validity for Shaw, as the basis of Marxism, and Bergson's notions seemed so congenial that Shaw claimed them for his own without even troubling to examine them. Fully committed as he was to an evolutionary pattern of change, it was natural for him to agree with Bergson that time is of the essence of being. After *Man and Superman* time plays a leading role in all Shaw's plays, but even in *Back to Methuselah* it is not definitely characterized: it is simply duration, the measure of the process through which the Will develops.

The consequence of the metaphysical attitudes which Shaw adapted to the stage was a view of man as a transitional phase in the development of a superior level of being, from which humanity as such might perhaps be ultimately excluded. The essential element in the characterization of Shaw's heroes is therefore their awareness of responsibility as agents of the Life Force, an entity which is not altogether distinguishable from the Hegelian *Weltgeist*. These characters are all, therefore, more or less conscious of a vocation in life to which all other considerations must be subordinated. This they have in common with Ibsen's great characters, from Brand to Rubek. But while Ibsen invariably stressed the sacrificial side of dedication and thus developed the tragedy of the engaged individual, Shaw magnified the cosmic element to the point where the individual's protest becomes, in the minuteness of its scale, an appropriate subject of comedy. In the crucial scene of *Man and Superman*, Tanner's personal uneasiness, as he surrenders to the onslaught of the Life Force in the guise of an attractive girl, is hardly calculated to make one weep in sympathy. He makes us grin. But Ibsen's John Gabriel is a deeply tragic figure, and in Brand, Rosmer, Solness, and Rubek there is not much that is funny.

Both Shaw and Ibsen were primarily comedic writers, typically concerned with the plight of the individual in his relation to society. If their drama is so widely dissimilar it is because of the different emphasis placed on the elements of the inner conflict their plays depict. In the interplay of psychic pressures, Shaw stressed the universal impulse as the significant reality, in relation to which the individual's concerns seem trivial. For Ibsen, however, drama was centered in the soul's loneliness. Beyond the individual consciousness there was only the unfathomable mystery of existence, of which nothing whatever could be said with confidence. For Ibsen drama took place in the individual; for Shaw the play of the individual was comprehensible only in terms of the universal comedy. The difference between them was thus chiefly a matter of scale.

Both were essentially skeptics. "In taking your side," Shaw had written, "don't trouble about its being the right side—north is no righter than South—but be sure that it is really yours, and then back it for all you're worth."

Shaw backed the Life Force for all he was worth. By 1903 he had apparently convinced himself that what he felt as an urgency within himself was the manifestation of a universal impulse which it was his high privilege to serve. This conviction gave him a delightful sense of freedom. The Life Force was, above all, original, and its originality was demonstrable in the behavior of those rare individuals who stood, like himself, in the forefront of the evolutionary process, and thus prefigured, at each stage in its development, the superhumanity of the future. From Shaw's viewpoint, these were the proper subjects of drama.

Since the Life Force is essentially dynamic and progressive, the superior individual is always at odds with a society that tends to perpetuate each stage of its career as if it were ultimate and eternal. The price of genius is incessant conflict; and the tension between the extraordinary individual and the mass of undifferentiated humanity he is destined to influence, though comic when viewed under the aspect of eternity, is in the temporal frame the subject of tragedy. God and the individual are in eternal opposition, while at the same time they are inseparable and completely interdependent expressions of one another. At the dawn of the twentieth century this paradox was neither new nor by any means peculiar to Shaw. Rilke was writing at about this time:

> Was wirst du tun, Gott, wenn ich sterbe?
> Ich bin dein Krug (wenn ich zerscherbe?)
> Ich bin dein Trank (wenn ich verderbe?)
> Bin dein Gewand und dein Gewerbe,
> mit mir verlierst du deinen Sinn.

Possibly in English:

> What wilt thou do, God, when I die?
> I am thy jug (when smashed am I?)
> I am thy drink (when I run dry?)
> Thy dress, thy trade—when I go hence
> wilt thou continue to make sense?

Shaw began working on *Man and Superman* in 1901. It took him two years to finish it and obviously it represented an enormous investment of creative energy. The reward was not immediate. Robert Loraine produced it successfully in New York in September 1905. In London The Stage

Society gave it two performances. Then on May 23, 1905, it opened a run of twelve matinees at the Royal Court with Granville-Barker as Tanner and Lillah McCarthy in the role of Ann Whitefield. The play was received with politeness, and the production was praised, but though the play had been in print for a year, in England the importance of *Man and Superman* was not yet generally apparent.

Man and Superman is subtitled *A Comedy and a Philosophy*. Of the two the comedy is by far the less interesting component. The plot is a love story, in Shaw's words, "a trumpery story of modern London life, a life in which, as you know, the ordinary man's main business is to get means to keep up the position and habits of a gentleman, and the ordinary woman's business is to get married." The result is a well-made play of conventional shape, founded upon a *méprise*, centered upon a love chase, embellished with melodramatic incidents involving brigands and rescuers, and resolved, in accordance with the usual tenets of romantic comedy, in the happy union of young lovers.

It is chiefly in the dream sequence of the third act that its symbolism becomes apparent. This act was considered dispensable even by the author. Yet it is John Tanner's dream, and only this, that gives the play its extraordinary scope and grandeur. The rest is, as Shaw indicated in the introduction, simply the story of the conquest of an eligible, but reluctant young man by a girl who has set her cap for him. The dream makes it clear that the play, as a whole, is a conceit intended to suggest the nature of the attraction that draws the sexes together—in short, an attempt to define love in cosmic terms.

The pattern of the action is conventionally Scribean. There are four acts, and, as usual in plays of this sort, two plots which converge toward the climax and are simultaneously resolved in the final scenes. The main plot is of the A loves B loves C variety and has the itinerant quality of romantic sequences traceable to the sixteenth-century epic. As in *Candida*, the heroine has a choice of men, but the heroine of *Man and Superman* makes a choice different from Candida's. She chooses the man who needs her least. For the rest, the situation is not markedly different from that of the earlier play. The poet, Tavy, is a pale reflection of Marchbanks. Tanner is a younger version of Morell. As between the two candidates for the hand of Ann it becomes evident that it is Tanner who is predestined to be the husband, while it is Tavy's lot to be the broken-hearted lover who creates poems instead of children. There is also Mendoza, his comic counterpart, the high quality of whose poetry it is possible to judge, since we are favored with a sample. He is evidently fated to be a brigand.

The *méprise* stems from the fact that, while Ann is supposedly in love with Tavy, who is solemnly warned against her wiles by Tanner, it is actually Tanner whom she is resolved to marry. This comes as a surprise to nobody except the men most nearly involved. When the situation is made clear to Tanner, however, he is terrified and makes off in his high-powered car, with Ann in hot pursuit. The chase takes them all halfway across Europe, to the Sierra Nevada in Spain. There Tanner is captured first by the brigand Mendoza, himself a hapless victim of love, and afterwards by Ann, who turns up with an armed escort and all the panoply of Eros, the police force and the Life Force.

The action could not be simpler. It is a love chase, the originality of which consists in the reversal of traditional roles. In this case, the lady is aggressive; the gentleman is coy; what gives the play its comic tone is that in this unconventional situation everyone tries to preserve appearances. The lady plays the coy maiden; and the gentleman, as the seemingly aggressive male, finds himself engaged in a rear-guard action against impossible odds.

In this play the main plot is concerned with courtship, the subplot with marriage; but there is little in it that can be called romantic. It is all extremely businesslike. Ann's sister Violet is supposedly bearing the child of an unknown lover, whose identity she refuses to disclose. In fact she is secretly married to Hector Malone, whose father opposes the match. It is the conquest of the father, and the father's millions, which principally occupies Violet; the conquest of Tanner is Ann's principal concern; and in the ruthless efficiency of the two young women in organizing their lives, the play makes its wry point: *amor omnia vincit*.

While *Man and Superman* is principally about love and marriage, it is also concerned with a closely related topic, the conflict of youth and age. The principal characters are all in their early twenties. "The Revolutionist's Handbook" appended to the play, as the work of John Tanner, is what one might expect from a bright young firebrand of the 1890s, and its radicalism inevitably conflicts with that of the still-smoking embers of an earlier age, such as Roebuck Ramsden. In the contrast between the former radical, who will not grasp the fact that the times have passed him by, and the young enthusiast, who is still somewhat ahead of his day, Shaw is able not only to indicate the relativism of accepted beliefs at successive stages of social evolution, but also to prefigure in the pathetic figure of the older man the sad destiny of the younger. The inevitable transformation of the fiery radicalism of each age into the pompous conservatism of the next is the natural order of a developing society. The contrasts are comic in their effect, but the implications of this dialectic are not altogether funny.

The contrast of generations, in the case of the ladies, is less emphatic, but no less striking. The female character, it is intimated, is more stable than the male, if only because her function in life is more clearly defined. Mrs. Whitefield, having fulfilled her role as mother, is no longer an agent of the Life Force, but her vital energy has passed in full measure to her daughter, Ann, whose femininity she fears, dislikes, and serves. The elderly Miss Ramsden, on the other hand, is the prototype of Violet, the supremely self-confident English gentlewoman, the backbone of the British Empire, the feminine principle upon which English manhood depends.

Shaw's purpose in juxtaposing the successive elements of a family history in this manner could not be more clear. In his view, the laws of heredity are irrefrangible. A chain of inexorable causation links each generation to the next. Just as the matrimonial choices of the generation that is departing have determined the shape of the generation that is taking its place, so the young people's love affairs of the moment are destined to shape the generation yet unborn. From the evolutionary viewpoint, love, the selective principle, is the essential biological determinant.

In the comedy of Tanner, Ann, and Tavy it is therefore possible to symbolize the eternal comedy of the husband, the lover, and the lady, and the triangle of romantic comedy is thus transformed into an exemplum of impressive magnitude. The situation in *Man and Superman* is assimilated to the myth of Don Juan, the legendary lover, in somewhat the same manner as James Joyce assimilated the itinerary of the peripatetic Mr. Bloom to the journeyings of Ulysses, the legendary wanderer. In the case of Shaw, also, the conceit is not especially apt, since the mythical Don Juan is an incorrigible philanderer, whereas John Tanner has no special interest in women, yet is fated for matrimony from the start. For Shaw's purposes, though, the analogy, however strained, was useful. John Tanner is what, in the course of evolution, Don Juan has become. The idea sprang, undoubtedly, from Shaw's experiences during the relatively brief period of his sexual flowering, the years from 1881 to 1898. Like *The Philanderer, Man and Superman* is both autobiographical and apologetic.

From what Shaw tells us of himself it seems plain that as a youth he was unusually susceptible. His early years were marked by a series of half-imaginary romantic attachments, the details of which are carefully posted in his diaries behind concealing asterisks, among notes of his engagements and current expenses. The painful shyness of his early twenties, his extensive poverty, and the morbid irritability which caused him to bicker periodically with the women he fancied kept him away from any serious involvement until the fateful evening in July 1885 when, on the occasion of his twenty-ninth birthday, Mrs. Jane Patterson induced him to spend the night in her house in Brompton Square. This initiated a period of amatory activity which Shaw never permitted himself or his public to forget.

"Jenny" Patterson was a widow some fifteen years his senior, quite wealthy, not especially beautiful, and of an unusually passionate and jealous disposition. She sang. Her relations with her singing teacher's son were for the most part stormy, but they were maintained over a period of fully seven years, a time marked by frequent and feverish displays of hysteria on her part, while her lover, on the other hand, hardly troubled to conceal his growing restlessness. In the meantime he worked assiduously at the complex system of interlocking flirtations with which he appears to have defended himself against the depredations of individual women while maintaining a receptive, and even aggressive, attitude toward the sex in general.

Of the half-dozen women with whom he achieved some intimacy during this time only Jenny Patterson seems to have involved him seriously. The nature of his amatory interests in this period is, of course, a matter of conjecture, but his state of mind is perhaps sufficiently indicated in a letter he wrote in October 1888 to Alice Lockett, a really pretty girl, judging by her photograph, with whom he had carried on a quarrelsome and fruitless love affair since first they met in 1881, when he was twenty-five:

> My season is commencing: my nights are filling up one by one. I am booked for a half-dozen lectures within the next month. I shall be out tonight with Stepniak and the underdone. My DR (Dramatic Review) copy must be done to-day, to-morrow an article is due for the Magazine of Music. On Saturday my contribution to Our Corner must be written. On Sunday there is a lecture ("The Attitude of Socialists Toward Other Bodies"), not one idea for which have I yet arranged. Meanwhile To-day is howling for more copy. See you this week! Avaunt, Sorceress: not this month—not until next July. Not, in any case, until I am again in the detestable humor which is the only one to which you minister. Remember, I am not always a savage. My pleasures are music, conversation, the grapple of my intelligence with fresher ones. All this I can sweeten with a kiss; but I cannot saturate and spoil it with fifty thousand. Love making grows tedious to me—the emotions have evaporated from it. This is your fault: since your return I have seen you twice, and both times you have been lazy and unintelligently luxurious. I will

not spend such evenings except when I am for a moment tired and brutish. . . . Do not forget that I cannot esteem the most beautiful woman for more than she is. I want as much as I can get; there is no need to force it upon me if it exists; I am only too thirsty for companionship. Beware. When all the love has gone out of me, I am remorseless: I hurl the truth about like destroying lightning. G.B.S.

Shaw cherished the belief all his life that he was interested in women primarily for literary purposes. The naïveté of this excuse for philandering need not obscure the ambiguity of Shaw's amatory proclivities, out of which he fashioned the doctrine of *Man and Superman*. Everything indicates that he was personally a most attractive man, witty, charming, amusingly unpredictable, but from a sexual viewpoint uncomfortably ambivalent. Like many men who are excessively aware of their talent, he was demanding in his relationships and frankly selfish in his aims. Married women principally interested him, or women who had been married: he evidently found the Candida situation particularly to his liking and reconstructed it among his acquaintances whenever he could. For all his ready fund of blarney, he was an essentially honest man and he made no secret of the fact that he had no intention of being trapped into matrimony, or even into lovemaking on any permanent basis. Even after he was married he declared, at least half-seriously, that he had been lured into domesticity only at the point of death.

The love letters he wrote Mrs. Patrick Campbell in 1913, when he was fifty-seven, are particularly revealing. It is clear that, while he longed for a passionate relationship with a woman that would fulfill his need for love, the prospect of a thorough physical involvement threw him into a panic, so that in almost every case his love affairs essentially amounted, as Mrs. Campbell noted, to "a carnival of words." It is possible that at this time he was sexually impotent, but his need for love was great. The letter that he wrote "Stella" in answer to an only mildly inflammatory letter from her, has, for all its rhetoric, an almost tragic tone:

Oh, if only you were alarmed, and could struggle, then I could struggle too. But to be gathered like a flower and stuck in your bosom frankly! to have no provocation to pursue, and no terror to fly! to have no margin of temptation to philander in! to have a woman's love on the same terms as a child's, to have nothing to seize, nothing to refuse, nothing to resist, everything for nothing . . . to draw the sword for the duel of sex with cunning confidence in practised skill and brass breastplate, and suddenly find myself in the arms of a mother—a young mother, and with a child in my own arms who is yet a woman; all this plunges me into the wildest terror. . . . Yet here I am caught up again, breathless, with no foothold, at a dizzy height, in an ecstasy which must be delirious and presently end in my falling headlong to destruction. And yet I am happy, as madmen are.

From the available facts, a psychologist might reasonably conjecture that in the women he courted Shaw sought, unconsciously, the unattainable mother of his infancy, the Virgin Mother around whom his fantasies unceasingly revolved. It is understandable, in these circumstances, that the establishment in adult life of a satisfactory sexual relationship was of prime importance to him, and also that he could not admit it as a possibility. In point of fact, whatever Shaw attempted along sexual lines seems to have been attended by profound feelings of guilt, and in the end he settled for a loveless marriage comfortably grounded upon friendship.

His courtship of Mrs. Pat Campbell was predicated on the knowledge that she was engaged to marry another and younger man. This fact only served to increase his ardor. He wrote her:

> I want my plaything that I am to throw away. I want my Virgin Mother enthroned in Heaven, I want my Italian peasant woman. I want my rapscalliony fellow-vagabond. I want my dark lady. I want my angel—I want my tempter. . . . I want my inspiration, my folly, my happiness, my divinity, my madness, my selfishness, my final sanity and sanctification, my transfiguration, my purification, my light across the sea, my palm across the desert, my garden of fresh flowers, my million nameless joys, my day's wage, my night's dream, my darling and my star.

Beyond any doubt there was a heartbreaking sincerity in the love letters Shaw wrote to Stella: it was his last chance at romance, and perhaps his first. But there was as much rhetoric in them as longing. It is impossible to say how much of Shaw's passion was mere literature. What is clear is the neurotic element in all of his philanderings, the desire to be overwhelmed and to suffer rather than to enjoy his loves. John Tanner exhibits unusual insight:

> Of all human struggles there is none so treacherous and remorseless as the struggle between the artist man and the mother woman. Which shall use up the other? that is the issue between them. And it is all the deadlier because, in your romanticist cant, they love one another.

The idea that an artist exploits the feelings of women in order to have something to write about has some savor of reason, but it is hardly realistic. The normal sexual curiosity of an adolescent may well be transformed into the professional voyeurism of the artist, but the idea that the dramatist makes love in order to write love scenes is less convincing than the idea that he writes plays in order to sublimate his lovemaking. In the case of *Man and Superman* it seems evident that the love story was not commensurate with the psychic needs of the author. It was necessary to supplement it with an elaborate philosophical system which would place the action on a plane of universality. Luckily, the material was at hand:

> The ultimate end of all love affairs, whether they are played in sock or cothurnus, is really more important than all other ends of human life, and is therefore quite worthy of the profound seriousness with which everyone pursues it. That which is decided by it is nothing less than *the composition of the next generation*. The *dramatis personae* who shall appear when we are withdrawn are here determined, both as regards their existence and their nature, by these frivolous love affairs.

This striking passage from the essay "Metaphysics of the Love of the Sexes," which Schopenhauer appended in 1844 to *The World as Will and Idea*, appears to have furnished the necessary basis for Shaw's metaphysics of sex in *Man and Superman*. The idea was, indeed, far-reaching in its implications. Schopenhauer had come under Eastern influence relatively early in his career. The Upanishads teach that a simple reality underlies the apparent multiplicity of the phenomenal world. The true self is not the individual consciousness, but the formless and voiceless being within each person, the impersonal spirit of life, the Atman. This divinity lies beyond the reach of the intellect, which is therefore powerless to arrive at the ultimate significance of being. It can be reached only by that final act of dissolution which comes with the relinquishing of both form and individuality, in short, in nirvana.

In accordance with this conception Schopenhauer advocated the view that individuality is an illusion, and that the individual will is simply a manifestation of the universal will. Man's intense preoccupation with love can therefore be justified on the basis of the imperiousness of the instinct through which the will to live combines the available biological forms so as to ensure the persistence of the species in its most perfect possible form. Schopenhauer wrote:

The will of the individual appears at a higher power as the will of the species . . . and what presents itself in the individual consciousness as sexual impulse in general . . . is simply the will to live. But what appears in consciousness as a sexual impulse directed to a definite individual is in itself the will to live as a definitely determined individual. Now in this case the sexual impulse, although in itself a subjective need, knows how to assume very skilfully the mask of an objective admiration, and thus to deceive our consciousness; for nature requires this stratagem to attain its ends.

In Schopenhauer's view, the future generation is

already active in that careful, definite, and arbitrary choice for the satisfaction of the sexual impulse which we call love. The growing inclination of two lovers is really already the will to live of the new individual which they can and desire to produce, a future individuality harmoniously and well composed. . . . They feel the longing for an actual union and fusing together into a single being in order to live on only as this; and this longing receives its fulfillment in the child which is produced by them, in which the qualities transmitted by them, fused and united in one being, live on.

Since the future child is a new Platonic idea, and "ideas strive with the greatest vehemence to enter the phenomenal world," the mutual passion of the future parents is simply the expression of the desire of the potential child to come into being. Schopenhauer saw the Will as chiefly operative in the father, and the intellect in the mother. Since the child's corporization comes from both parents, the degree of harmony in these elements is the measure of the attraction between the individuals who embody them. "The more perfect the mutual adaptation of two individuals to each other . . . the stronger will be their mutual passion," while aversion is the sign of an inharmonious set of physical and mental qualities.

In these biological combinations the individual actually counts for little: "Egotism is deeply rooted—but the species has a greater claim on the individual than the perishable individuality itself." Since nature strives to maintain in the progeny a mean between the extreme manifestations of sexual differences, it is natural for manly men to seek out womanly women as their mates. The lover imagines that in his choice he serves his own inclinations. In fact he is serving the interest of the species "which presents what is of benefit to it to the will which is here become individual." Thus the individual is actually the dupe of the species, insofar as its interests differ from his own; and what he experiences as love is no more than his sense of the suitability of his mate to join with him in procreating, as well as possible, the being which is to be produced.

In the 1890s, when these ideas had percolated English thought, the question of love and marriage came once again under careful scrutiny. A number of radical writers, among them Belfort Bax, Edward Carpenter, Grant Allen, and Havelock Ellis, took up the cudgels for a rational approach to the problems of sex. Schopenhauer's idea of love as a manifestation of the unconscious wisdom of the species now became the basis for a full-scale discussion of eugenics, and the desirability of accelerating the evolutionary process through artificial selection. The group that called itself neo-Malthusian publicized the idea that poverty was the result of indiscriminate breeding. Grant Allen and Havelock Ellis both argued that inequalities of class and wealth put unnecessary obstacles in the way of eugenic marriages, and Belfort Bax—a Marxist and an ardent Schopenhauerian—published a series of papers advocating the regulation of marriage, divorce, and birth control from the viewpoint of social policy rather than that of property and religion.

The effect of these discussions was to emphasize more and more strongly the role of women in carrying on what Schopenhauer had called "the affairs of the species." In an essay translated by Bax in 1891, Schopenhauer had written: "It lies therefore in the nature of women to regard everything solely as a means to win the man, the interest in anything else being never more than a simulated one."

It was evidently from such sources that Shaw derived the theoretical basis of Man and Superman. Schopenhauer provided whatever was needed to formulate a love story as "scientific natural history"; but evidently in Shaw's estimation, this theory did not account properly for all the facts. Schopenhauer subordinated everything in the love story to the urge for producing children. In his view the unborn child, as Idea, presided over each sexual union, and the child's insistence on being brought into being was the source of the urgency and intensity of the lovers' passion. Thus far, the metaphysics of sex was acceptable to Shaw, but Shaw was an individualist who thought of himself as an amatory freebooter. He had no desire to beget progeny and found the deterministic tendency of Schopenhauer's doctrine oppressive. Before this system became entirely acceptable to him it was necessary that the will to live be reconciled with the freedom to philander.

The image of Don Juan provided the necessary means. Don Juan is the culture hero who best embodies for our time the idea of freedom without responsibility. He is the archetypal philanderer, eternally available, and eternally inconstant, resisting no temptation save the temptation to be localized in marriage.

The original Don Juan, as Tirso de Molina conceived him, is of quite another sort. He is a prankster who plays practical jokes, and whose ambition it is to be thought the greatest trickster in Spain. He is not a lover of women, but the contrary of a lover. His sexual exploits are athletic, aggressive, and cruel, a form of manly prowess which is at the other pole from the ways of true love. He is, in fact, the seventeenth-century version of the medieval *losengier*, a deceiver who apes the lover in order to gain his ends, and it is his special pleasure to dishonor women. As Tamburlaine was the scourge of kings, sent by heaven to humble their pride, Don Juan is the scourge of women and serves a similar purpose. It is appropriate that he is damned for his pains.

Shaw did not have this figure in mind. His Don Juan belongs to a later age and plainly shows the influence of Molière. He is a romantic figure, a rebel who refuses to be bound by convention, dominated by his passions and determined to have his will at any cost. Shaw evidently found this figure fascinating. In the great cynic, duelist, and wit, particularly in the operatic form which Mozart had given him, Shaw doubtless saw much of himself, and in his early life he made valiant efforts to emulate this irresistible figure. In the Epistle Dedicatory to *Man and Superman* he gives evidence of having researched the subject thoroughly. He mentions all the major versions of the myth from *El Burlador de Sevilla* to *Don Giovanni*, all, that is, but the one most apposite to his purpose, Zorilla's *Don Juan Tenorio* (1844). There is, however, a certain difference between the romantic figure which Da Ponte devised for Mozart's opera and Shaw's Don Juan. In Shaw's view Don Juan is not an exploiter of women. He is their victim.

The turn given to the Don Juan myth in *Man and Superman* developed the theme of a short story which Shaw had written a dozen years earlier, in 1887. In this story, entitled "Don Juan Explains," the ghost of Don Giovanni appears to the narrator in a railway carriage in order, as he says, to correct through him the current misconception of his character and purposes. Don Giovanni begins by explaining that, while his friends considered him devoid of moral fiber, he was in truth an exceptionally evolved individual who, having come into existence long before his time, was not properly appreciated by his contemporaries. In fact, he was a preternaturally shy young man whose sexual maturity was deferred until at last a widowed lady threw herself into his arms and conquered his timidity so far as to permit him to possess her. Unhappily, after a month with this lady, he found the romantic side of the affair "tedious, unreasonable and even, except at rare moments, forced and insincere." This uncomfortable indoctrination into the mysteries of love rendered him immune to the attraction of sex. Neither Doña Ana nor Zerlina interested him in the least, and his passion for Elvira was simply a figment of her imagination. After his experience with the statue of the Commander, he was dragged off to a hell made up of well-intentioned nonentities who despised the saints in heaven as unfeeling snobs of frightfully boring character and disposition.

One needs no great acumen to locate the autobiographical elements in this story. The relation to the scene in hell in *Man and Superman* is equally clear. These identifications have a certain importance. They justify the inference that Don Juan in Hell essentially represents Shaw in hell, and that the dialogue with the Devil and the Statue is interpretable as a transcription of the author's inner debate with regard to issues of the deepest personal interest.

In Tanner's vision, hell is an eternity of pleasure. It is peopled by such souls as prefer to live in a state of perpetual illusion, bemused by such idle fancies as youth, beauty, love, and romance, together with the arts through which such fantasies are given a semblance of reality. This aesthetic dream world is fittingly presided over by the master illusionist, the Devil. To those who prefer reality, however, an eternity of pleasure is an eternity of boredom, the worst of all possible torments. For these elect, salvation is to be found only in the useful expenditure of energy, that is, in work. Heaven, accordingly, is a state of constant striving.

In a program note written by Shaw for the first performance of *Don Juan in Hell* at the Court Theatre on June 4, 1907, he explained that

> modern theology conceives heaven and hell, not as places, but as states of the soul; and by the soul it means, not an organ like the liver, but the divine element common to all life, which causes us "to do the will of God" in addition to looking after our individual interests, and to honor one another solely for our divine activities and not at all for our selfish activities.

This "higher theology" moreover, held that

> this world, or any other, may be made a hell by a society so lacking in the higher orders of energy that it is given wholly to the pursuit of immediate individual pleasure, and cannot even

conceive the passion of the divine will. Also that any world can be made a heaven by a society of persons in whom that passion is the master passion, "a communion of saints" in fact.

The identification of the Schopenhauerian Will with the divine principle, and the assimilation of the *état d'âme* of the individual with the condition of society at a given time, had already been made in the prefatory material published with *Man and Superman* in 1901. This preface was in the form of a dedicatory letter addressed to A. B. Walkley who, after having seen service on the *Speaker*, the *Observer*, and the *Star*, had lately taken over the post of drama critic on the *Times* and was in this period the most discriminating and most respected theater critic in England. The Epistle Dedicatory went some way beyond dedication. It not only fathered the play upon Walkley, it also involved him tacitly in its ideology on the basis *qui facit per alium facit per se*.

It was characteristic of Shaw to confer intellectual partnership upon people whose opinions he valued, particularly with regard to ideas that stood in some need of support. The connection between Walkley and *Man and Superman* was largely imaginary. In 1902 there had appeared a volume of Walkley's collected articles which included a review, written in February 1890, of John Buchanan's version of a French dramatization of *Clarissa Harlowe*. In this article Walkley had written, apropos of the characterization of Lovelace:

> No doubt the Don Juans of real life are often poor, empty creatures. Women have strange taste. But if you bring a Don Juan on the stage, you must make him a Don Juan who satisfies my imagination. There must be a magnificence about the fellow; he must be a virtuoso in the Fine Art of Don Juanism; must have *maestria*: must be a philosopher like the Don Juan of Molière; a heroic figure that will not make Leporello's catalogue sound ridiculous; a host not too puny to invite the statue of the commander to supper. How else will you satisfy a generation that (if it does not read "Clarissa Harlowe") is very familiar with Feuillet's M. de Camors and Daudet's Duc de Mora? I recognize the dramatist's difficulty here. A character of this complexity is not easily rendered by the simple method of the stage.

It is possible that Shaw had this passage in mind in connecting his Don Juan play with Walkley. The Epistle Dedicatory of *Man and Superman* begins with the remark that Walkley had once asked Shaw why he did not write

a Don Juan play. After considering with some archness the various implications of this question, which he interprets as a request, Shaw decides that
what Walkley required of him was "a Don Juan in the philosophic sense."
Philosophically, Don Juan is "a man who, though gifted enough to be
exceptionally capable of distinguishing between good and evil, follows his
own instincts without regard to the common, statute, or canon law . . .
and therefore . . . finds himself in moral conflict with existing
institutions. . . ."

These institutions, he continues, are no longer those of the sixteenth
or the eighteenth century, but the beliefs of the ubiquitous middle class, as
a result of which women of all classes have become equally dangerous, so
that, if they are wronged, "they grasp formidable legal and social weapons,
and retaliate. . . . As a result,

> Man is no longer, like Don Juan, victor in the duel of sex. . . .
> His thousand and three affairs of gallantry, after becoming, at
> most, two immature intrigues leading to sordid and prolonged
> complications and humiliations, have been discarded altogether
> as unworthy of his philosophic dignity. . . . Instead of pretend-
> ing to read Ovid he does actually read Schopenhauer and
> Nietzsche, studies Westermarck, and is concerned for the future
> of the race instead of for the freedom of his own instincts. . . .
> he is now more Hamlet than Don Juan.

Through this line of reasoning Shaw manages somehow to relate Don
Juan's legendary exploits to his own relatively modest achievements as a
philanderer and thus arrives at a conception of the arch-seducer as one more
sinned against than sinning. In *The Philanderer* Shaw does not make out a
very strong case for Charteris as a lover of women, nor does he do much
better for Valentine, the sex duelist in *You Never Can Tell*. It is in *Man and
Superman* that these characters are finally developed, and here, for the first
time, the pursuer turns out to be the pursued. The difficulty with the
characterization is, however, that while Charteris and Valentine are both
depicted as woman-chasers, John Tanner gives no indication of being at all
interested in the opposite sex.

The ingenious turn upon which *Man and Superman* depends was doubtless suggested by Shaw's own sense of being ruthlessly hounded by adoring
females. It was a feeling—judging by his diaries—barely supported by the
facts, but one which he evidently cherished and strove mightily to realize
in his manifold flirtations with Fabian ladies. From Shaw's viewpoint, Don
Juan is a man irresistible to women, who occasionally condescends to one

or another while he keeps his mind resolutely fixed on the higher things of life.

Apart from the similarity of their names, it is difficult to see what John Tanner has to do with Don Juan Tenorio in Zorilla's play, or in Mozart's opera. It is with astonishment that we learn in act 1 of *Man and Superman* that in some mysterious manner Tanner is descended from Don Juan, and even when we realize that their relationship is purely spiritual, the analogy seems strained. In fact, Don Juan, as he appears in hell, represents only the fugitive aspect of John Tanner; the rest of the similitude we must take on faith. In John Fletcher's comedy *The Wild Goose Chase* (1621), it is the hero's elusiveness which makes him especially attractive to the ladies of the play. It is certainly not Tanner's recalcitrance which appeals to Ann Whitefield. It is his forthright maleness that attracts her, while the soft romanticism of Tavy makes him, in her opinion, undesirable as a mate.

Tavy has only the vaguest relation to Don Ottavio in the Mozart opera. Like Marchbanks in *Candida*, he is not marriageable. He is the eternally frustrated lover, the poet who idealizes, but never possesses the lady, a vestige of the Petrarchan tradition. It is his destiny to create works of art, not children, and it is precisely because he never possesses the lady that he is able to idealize her in his fantasy. John Tanner, on the other hand, has no illusions about the lady in question. He sees through her wiles perfectly in everything save what concerns himself and, believing himself to be immune from her machinations, he thinks only of protecting his friend. This is not the cream of the jest. The practical joke, of which he is the victim, is of cosmic magnitude.

Tanner is not, like Hector Malone, *l'homme moyen sensuel*, whose business in life is merely to perpetuate the species on its present cultural level. He is a superior being, intellectually advanced and physically apt above the other men in his circle, and he appeals to Ann for reasons more cogent than she knows. He attracts her precisely because, whether she is aware of it or not, it is his child she desires to create, one who will bring the species a step closer to its entelechy. Therefore she hastens to unite with him in obedience to high behests, which she heeds without in the least identifying them, and is willing to sacrifice everything to bring about this union—her modesty, her integrity, even, if need be, her life.

Tanner is the darling of the Life Force and for that reason destined for sacrifice. In the cut of his mind, and the cut of his clothes, he serves as a modern counterpart of that *kalokágathia* which the ancients prized in their young men. He is strong, but in the hands of the implacable power that preempts his energies, he is helpless. His position thus approximates that of the tragic hero of classic drama, and if we are disposed to laugh at his plight instead of feeling the appropriate measure of pity and terror, it is only partly because we lack imagination. In our social framework, marriage with a pretty woman cannot really be considered a fate worse than death, and the fact that Tanner sees the matter in this light gives a comic turn to a situation which on another scale might well fulfill the conditions of tragedy.

It is doubtless in order to suggest this higher level of interpretation that the Dialogue in Hell precedes the scene in the garden—one might say of Eden—in which the sacrifice of Tanner is celebrated. The upshot, as in *Candida*, is an interpretation of the age-old story of the wife, the lover, and the husband in a manner that seems original with Shaw. In his view, the cosmic Will asserts its biologic choices through the female, so that every woman knows instinctively the man best fitted by nature to serve her procreative function. The artist, the thinker, the poet—self-engrossed, meditative types primarily interested in creative activity along intellectual or aesthetic lines—are parthenogenetic organisms not properly fitted for the task of bisexual procreation. The woman may find such men to her liking, but in her instinctive wisdom, she rejects them no matter how attractive they may seem. Nor is the ordinary man much to her liking, though she may have to settle for him, for she can do no more than to perpetuate his mediocrity. The truly desirable man is one who is developed beyond the generality, but not to the point where he is beyond the possibility of domestication. Such is John Tanner. In him, as Mrs. Whitefield remarks, Ann meets her match.

For Strindberg also, marriage was a form of martyrdom, but the purpose of marriage, as he saw it, was quite other than eugenic reproduction. In *To Damascus*, and *The Dream Play*, and in *The Dance of Death*, marriage is the refining flame through which the spirit is purified. Shaw takes another view of the matter. Tanner's martyrdom is real enough, but the dance into which Ann leads him is not the dance of death. It is the dance of life. His agony is measured by the extent to which the life to which marriage condemns him falls short of the ideal existence of which he dreams, but his sufferings are by no means unendurable. "I never was master in my own house, sir," the Waiter tells Valentine at the end of *You Never Can Tell*. "My wife was like your young lady: she was of a commanding and masterful disposition, which my son has inherited. But if I had my life to live twice over, I'd do it again, I assure you."

In Shaw's view, the good life is a constant labor and is consequently never a happy experience. Happiness implies stasis, which negates the vital principle. Heaven is a state of eternal dissatisfaction. Presumably the blissful moment which will lure Tanner into crying *"Verweile doch!"* will thrust him instantly into hell. For the dedicated revolutionist in particular domestic happiness constitutes a mortal danger. Shaw's attitude in this regard was not especially original. "He that is unmarried," St. Paul admonishes, "careth for the things that belong to the Lord, how he may please the Lord, but he that is married careth for the things that are of this world, how he may please his wife."

In this manner Shaw, after a prolonged detour through the most advanced thought of his day, found a safe harbor in the traditional tenets of his youth. His aspiring geniuses, the Marchbanks, Dudgeons, and Brassbounds—to say nothing of the saints who already populate his heaven—are humanity's priests and, by reason of their vocation, are exempt from carnal involvements. They are, at most, philanderers, lovers for whom woman is a point of departure, never a stopping place. So it was with Don Juan also; and now, like the archetypal lover of the *Symposium*, he desires to relinquish the delights of hell.

The denizens of his hell are romantics, diligently torturing themselves in the endless pursuit of pleasure; but Don Juan has found no happiness in pleasure. Happiness, as Aristotle noted, "does not lie in amusement; it would, indeed, be strange if the end were amusement, and one were to take trouble and suffer hardship all one's life in order to amuse oneself." Don Juan's horror at the prospect of an eternity of pleasure corresponds to the misgivings of a highly evolved individual in this life who has nothing to do but to amuse himself as long as he lives. For such a man happiness is an impossible will-o'-the-wisp. The alternative is the quest for blessedness, the realistic substitute for happiness. It is this which Don Juan, like Marchbanks, hopes to find among those who are engaged in the eternal life of contemplation that is their heaven.

The Dialogue in Hell is obviously meant to be read metaphorically. It takes place in the mind of man, specifically in the mind of a certain man and is, in this sense, autobiographical. In the critical position in which Tanner is placed at the end of the second act, he finds himself torn by contrary impulses, doubts, and fears. It is this state of mental turmoil which the dream sequence represents. In the portion of *Man and Superman* which takes place on the plane of contemporary reality, this critical moment is effectively dramatized in terms of freedom and the loss of individuality. But in the aspect of eternity the problem of marriage is seen to center on much wider issues, on the nature of men and the purpose of life.

Practically the discussion in hell involves the choice between the carefree life of the senses, self-justified, and a life of intellectual labor, justified by an ideal. The alternatives had long ago been allegorized as "The Choice of Hercules," the subject of a celebrated painting by Rubens, and it had furnished Carlyle also with a congenial theme. In *Man and Superman* the Devil is a romantic. He speaks eloquently for the sensual life. Don Juan argues for the life of the intellect. Neither is the victor, for the issue is beyond resolution, and the conflict is never-ending.

In hell there are no hard facts, only agreeable enchantments. It is a *locus amoenus* of the order of the Bower of Bliss or the Garden of Armida, a pleasant place to be, but bad for the soul: one would imagine hell was Shaw's idea of a resort hotel on the Riviera. Heaven, on the contrary, is a never-ending contemplation of reality. Unlike the sensual life, which is aimless, the life of the mind has a goal. It aims at the extension of knowledge; it represents the desire of life to know itself. It is to the furtherance of this taste that Don Juan, having grown weary of pleasure, now resolves to devote his eternity. These activities, the Statue remarks, are not universally amusing. They require a special aptitude, which he no longer shares. He himself has decided, after a long sojourn in heaven, to spend some aeons in hell.

Between these two spirits who meet at the crossroads of the infinite— the Statue who is bored with heaven, and the sensualist who is weary of hell—the Devil plays an equivocal role. He is a suave and convincing personage, well-suited to manage the sort of luxury hotel which hell seems to be, and naturally anxious not to lose his clientele to the competition. Doña Ana is no match, intellectually speaking, for these gentlemen among whom her lot is cast, but she is impressively single-minded: she is eternally in search of fruition. Doña Ana belongs neither to heaven nor to hell. She embraces both. As the vehicle of life she is neutral and anonymous, but indispensable.

The Devil has no use for Doña Ana, but Don Juan sees clearly that squalling brats and household chores are the price humanity must pay for the perpetuation of the race. The Statue adds that a life without responsibility, while seemingly attractive, leads only to an endless demand for entertainment, and at last to the discomforts of old age and impotence. As an ancient hedonist, he himself has amply experienced the disadvantages of the sensual life. "I confess," he remarks, "that if I had nothing to do in the world but wallow in these delights I should have cut my throat." In these circumstances, his decision to settle in hell does not seem particularly logical. But the Devil understands it. Men tire of everything, he says, of heaven no less than hell. History is nothing but the record of the oscillations of the human spirit between these extremes. Under the aspect of eternity, Don Juan and the Statue continually change places, for Don Juan will weary of the life of reason just as surely as he has wearied of the life of pleasure. What appears to be progress is nothing but change, and all that can be said of this is *"vanitas vanitatum."* Life has neither aim, nor end.

It is at this point in the discussion that Don Juan loses patience, for the hit is shrewd. He has an answer. If life has no purpose, one will be found. The Life Force has devised consciousness in order to know itself. It is even now at work developing means for discovering its purpose and its destiny. The means is the philosophic mind. The philosopher is nature's pilot, "And there you have our difference," Juan tells the Devil, "To be in hell is to drift: to be in heaven is to steer." The Devil answers: "On the rocks, most likely." To which Don Juan answers: "Pooh! which ship goes oftenest on the rocks or to the bottom—the drifting ship or the ship with a pilot on board?" In the absence of precise statistics, the question remains unresolved; but the indication is that Don Juan means to take a course in navigation: he proposes to spend eternity in developing his mind.

The Devil sees no reason to develop the human mind any further. Man has shown himself, he points out, chiefly ingenious in devising means of destruction. What best captures his imagination is not life but death: "There is nothing in Man's industrial machinery but his greed and sloth: his heart is in his weapons. This marvellous force of Life of which you boast is a force of Death: Man measures his strength by his destructiveness." In our day, nearly three-quarters of a century after *Man and Superman* was written, the Devil's argument seems even more cogent than it was when it was first propounded:

> Nowadays the chronicles describe battles. In a battle two bodies of men shoot at one another with bullets and explosive shells until one body runs away. . . . Over such battles the people run about the streets yelling with delight, and egg their governments on to spend hundreds of millions of money in the slaughter, whilst the strongest Ministers dare not spend an extra penny in the pound against the poverty and pestilence through which they themselves daily walk.

The argument, however, does not unsettle Don Juan. He answers that, while men seem to be bold and bad, they are really cowards and will undergo every humiliation in order to live. Man becomes heroic only in the service of an idea: "I tell you, gentlemen, if you can shew a man a piece of what he calls God's work to do, and what he will later on call by many new names, you can make him entirely reckless of the consequences to him personally." The task of the saints is, accordingly, the creation of ideas for men to live by, vital ideas. It is to this work that Don Juan proposes to devote his energies. The transition from hell is simple. When we think, we are in heaven. The Devil, for his part, wishes him joy of his undertaking. His reward will be, "in a word, the punishment of the fool who pursues the better before he has secured the good." Don Juan replies, "But at least I shall not be bored. The service of the Life Force has that advantage, at all events."

Thus Don Juan and the Devil part company in a manner reminiscent of the scene toward the end of Strindberg's *To Damascus III* (1901), and they leave Doña Ana to vanish by herself in the void. She has just acquired an idea. She has overheard the Devil remark that to the superman—something conceived by a German-Polish madman named Nietzsche—the human race will seem an inferior species. Her mission suddenly becomes clear to her and, as she vanishes, she cries, apparently to the universe, "A father! a father for the Superman!"

On this note the dialogue ends. It is perhaps not entirely satisfactory from the viewpoint of philosophy, but it is beyond doubt a great masterpiece of English literature. It might seem that Don Juan's decision should hang on something more solid than the thought that an eternity of work is the only alternative to an eternity of boredom. But the *taedium vitae* he fears is a more potent threat to the Life Force than any other. Boredom is the one illness the will to live cannot survive. The final argument helps also to justify Shaw's position as a realist—and also Don Juan's—for his line of reasoning brings him very close to an idealistic conclusion, and he has no way of disproving historically the Devil's paraphrase of Ecclesiastes. To the observation that all is vanity an honest man can oppose nothing but the faith which perhaps in time moves mountains.

Ann and Superman: Type and Archetype

Sally Peters Vogt

Despite the voluminous criticism devoted to *Man and Superman*, Ann Whitefield, Shaw's most persuasively feminine heroine, continues to be an enigma. Most critics would agree with Arthur H. Nethercot that Ann is Shaw's "prototype of predatory females," but assessments of her specific role vary. Thus Barbara Bellow Watson celebrates Ann's vitality and originality; Margery M. Morgan denounces her calculating conventionality; and Elsie Adams finds that Ann is merely "a composite of traditional types" of heroines. Nor is this surprising, since within the play itself Ann appears in many guises, so that her fellow *dramatis personae* perceive her from their own narrowly circumscribed perspectives. But while the characters' restricted views of Ann provide a major source of the comedy, a coherent assessment of her role requires a broader viewpoint that will discern the genesis of apparent discrepancies in her characterization.

Curiously, the implicitly mythic nature underlying much of the dramatic action has been largely ignored, although a number of studies have focused on the relation between the Don Juan legend and the play. Yet Shaw's use of both the Don Juan legend and his philosophy of Creative Evolution is an ordering of once powerful mythic patterns that, even though now attenuated, continue to survive and function in the modern world. Once the presence and function of these mythic patterns are revealed, Ann's role will be clarified. It will then be possible to assess the ways in which

From *Fabian Feminist: Bernard Shaw and Woman*, edited by Rodelle Weintraub. © 1977 by The Pennsylvania State University. The Pennsylvania State University Press, 1977.

Ann is a typical, and not so typical, Victorian heroine, and the ways in which her role demands archetypal formulation. Since Ann's characterization suspends from mythic elements, this dimension of *Man and Superman* will be explored in an effort to uncover the ultimate face behind Ann's many masks. While all four acts of the play will be considered, it is in the crucial third act that mythic elements are most clearly discernible.

That Shaw was aware of and sympathetic to the possibilities of myth is evident from both his admiration of Wagner and his symbolic reading of *The Ring* in *The Perfect Wagnerite*, a reading that supports Shaw's own evolutionary view. Underlying this affinity to myth is Shaw's essentially religious nature, which manifested itself in his lifelong evangelicalism. Shaw's devotion to his own particular view, however, did not prevent him from recognizing basic similarities between diverse phenomena that function as hierophanies, that is, to reveal what is "sacred" to the believer. In the preface to the *Plays Pleasant* he can thus assert of the times:

> Religion was alive again, coming back upon men, even upon clergymen, with such power that not the Church of England itself could keep it out. Here my activity as a Socialist had placed me on sure and familiar ground. To me the members of the Guild of St. Matthew were no more "High Church clergymen," Dr Clifford no more "an eminent Nonconformist divine," than I was to them "an infidel." There is only one religion, though there are a hundred versions of it. We all had the same thing to say; and though some of us cleared our throats to say it by singing revolutionary lyrics and republican hymns, we thought nothing of singing them to the music of Sullivan's Onward Christian Soldiers or Haydn's God Preserve the Emperor.

A hundred versions of one religion—this is the view of the comparative religionist and the cultural anthropologist. Shaw's version emerges in the harmonies of Creative Evolution scored for both virtuoso performance and background music in *Man and Superman*. Inquiry into this implicitly mythic and religious play can be enriched by a widening of critical perspective, so that our range of vision more closely approximates Shaw's. Consequently, in order to reevaluate Ann, the mythic dimension of the play will be explored, using the insights of scholars who approach myth from the viewpoints of the history of religions (Mircea Eliade), anthropology (Joseph Campbell), psychology (Carl G. Jung), symbolism (J. E. Cirlot) and literary criticism (Northrop Frye). In addition, these insights will facilitate a wider frame of reference in describing certain formal properties of the play.

It is noteworthy at the outset that the action of
located in two different structures: the immediately a
face reveals the familiar action of comic romance, w
suing and pursued characters; this in turn derives f
structure, mythic in both content and origin, whos
the surface action. The two structures, therefore, do not mere,
they are hierarchically related, with the second grounding the first. But the
specific relationships between the two are by no means self-evident. In fact,
it is precisely the reduction and deletion of much of the overtly mythic
material in three of the four acts that has led to the apparently anomalous
surface form of the play. Thus, in acts 1, 2 and 4, the romantic comedy of
Ann's pursuit of John Tanner is so much to the fore that the mythic deep
structure appears to be, if not entirely eliminated, then at least largely
submerged. Conversely, in the crucial third act, the formerly latent deep
structure surfaces with almost startling clarity, while the action of the romantic comedy is held in abeyance. Both these structures must be understood and explicitly correlated, if Ann is to emerge in her totality, and if
the pattern behind the woman-dominated, woman-motivated dramatic action is to be clearly perceived.

Before the underlying mythic pattern and Ann's place in this pattern
can be revealed, however, we must first examine the familiar surface structure. Female domination of the male is one of the most obvious characteristics of the surface structure, a truly remarkable paradox since the women
have no outlet for their energies outside their narrowly and traditionally
defined social and biological roles. Biology is indeed destiny in the not
always comic world of Ann Whitefield and Violet Robinson. Nevertheless,
within the confines of their roles, these women exert a powerful, though
always decorous force. The consequence is remarkable: *the men are defined
through their relationships with women.* Thus, despite Tanner's protests against
marriage and his pretensions to being a utopian philosopher, we view him
as a frightened male fleeing from Ann. Similarly, Roebuck Ramsden may
be a "president of highly respectable men," as the stage directions inform
us, but we see only what Ann calls "Annie's Granny," a pompous and
ineffectual man. Just as Ramsden is rendered powerless by his myopic view
of Ann, so the aspiring poet Octavius is paralyzed by a romanticized conception of Ann, which pervades all his speeches and actions.

But Ann is not the only strong woman in the play. Both Hector
Malone, Sr. and his son are dominated by Violet's desire to have money
as well as marriage—Malone Jr. at the outset; Malone Sr. finally. Nor, as
we discover in the dream frame, must the women necessarily be present

shape their men's lives. Unrequited love for the absent Louisa has made a mountain brigand out of the urbane waiter Mendoza. Romantic longing impels Mendoza to reveal his love to the supremely rational Henry Straker. As the long arm of comic coincidence would have it, Straker is Louisa's brother, and Mendoza's news strips him of rationality, goading him into an emotional reaction at odds with his scientific outlook. In hell, of course, what we already know of Don Juan, and what we will know, centers on his former susceptibility to and present disdain of feminine charms.

Since women exercise such powerful role-defining influence, it is perfectly consistent that the surface structure of the comedy charts Tanner's reactions to women in great detail. In one sense, woman-initiated thought or action is responsible for all the actions, physical and discursive, of Tanner and Don Juan. Thus the entire first act shows Tanner in a series of reactions, first to Ann's insistence on retaining him as her guardian, second in his embarrassing defense of Violet, and finally in his confession to Ann of "the birth in [him] of moral passion." Tanner, in his reactive role, has much in common with the passive hero of melodrama. The stupid conventionalism of the melodramatic hero becomes, paradoxically, converted in Tanner into the opaque brilliance of a would-be revolutionist uttering panegyrics on the Life Force.

Act 2 shows Ann adroitly manipulating Tanner, who, in response, leaps into "a sociological rage," only to be neatly deflated. Not yet daunted, Tanner replies with the outrageous challenge that Ann race across Europe with him; she stuns him by accepting. Once he learns from Straker of Ann's matrimonial inclinations, Tanner is forced into a frantic dash from her in hopes of preserving his single state. But Ann successfully pursues him into the Sierra Nevadas; even while yelling "Caught!" he continues to react against the idea of marriage, not verbally acquiescing until the very end of act 4. Still he valiantly tries to persuade himself and his auditors that he is in command of the hour, precisely, though fruitlessly, outlining his spartan terms for the marriage ceremony and its accoutrements. Unruffled, Ann assures him that he should "go on talking," to which Tanner can only indignantly sputter "Talking!"—his final reaction to Ann and, fittingly, the final speech of *Man and Superman*.

It is obvious, therefore, that in the surface structure of the romantic comedy, women not only influence but actually control the action. Though stoutly fending off marriage until the very end of the play, Tanner speaks of the inevitability of his reaction by alluding, in Schopenhauerian terms, to the intangible force that directs men's lives: "We do the world's will, not our own." Thus Tanner's reactions culminate in his engagement to

Ann because, as he so deterministically puts it, "It is the world's will that [Ann] should have a husband."

Just as the surface structure of the romantic comedy is a comic inversion of the pursuit of the heroine by the hero, so the dramatically slender surface of the dream symposium revolves around the comic inversion of the Don Juan theme. Don Juan, the arch libertine, becomes the pursued prey who seeks only a meditative respite from the rigors of ever-pursuing, ever-amorous women. Because of a duel over a woman Don Juan is in hell, and even there Woman continues to direct his destiny, a result of having on earth "interpreted all the other teaching" for him, consequently revealing the extent of his susceptibility to irrational life. Thus, in a perverse parody of Descartes' *cogito ergo sum*, he confesses, "It was Woman who taught me to say 'I am; therefore I think.' And also 'I would think more; therefore I must be more.' "

On one level, then, the play seems to exist merely to dramatize Shaw's joke about women who pursue. Much of the humor of the joke lies in Shaw's manipulation of conventional melodramatic roles. As an example of type, Ann resembles the heroine less than she does the siren of melodrama, but high passion has been channeled into its single respectable course, which leads—however lively the wooing—to marriage. Part of the waywardness Ann radiates can therefore be attributed to the tension resulting from the intertwining of two radically different melodramatic types: the intriguing siren and the forever chaste heroine. Consequently, Ann appears fascinating to those who admire energetic clever women, or hypocritical to those who are shocked by the covert operation of the marriage trap.

An analysis of the deep structure of the play, however, eliminates the need for such either/or judgments, since it becomes apparent that the complexities engendered by Ann's multiple guises are grounded in her universal-mythic role. This role may at first be difficult to discern, for the play's cosmic focus has been blurred by the use of the traditional, albeit inverted, romantic comedy. The action of the romantic comedy stems, nevertheless, from a mythic base. Ironically, the dialectical structure of the dream symposium (heaven versus hell, reality versus illusion, optimism versus pessimism) has had a similar obscurantist function: first because of its ambiguous relationship to the rest of the play; second because its brilliant rhetoric attracts attention to *lexis*, not *praxis*, verbal meaning seemingly overwhelming any function as action this rhetoric might serve. Shaw's brilliant display in the dream symposium is not mere pyrotechnics, however, but is rooted in a fundamental mythic rhythm. The organizing rhythm of dialectic is, as Frye has shown, as basic a unifying pattern as the cyclical rhythm customarily encountered in mythic works. Thus the major phases of human experience revealed by the action—birth and death, initiation and marriage—are set against the moral dialectic which pits the affirmative Life Force against the negating ignorance and vice of the world. And since unending dialectic is but another name for process, and since process is the essence of Creative Evolution, Shaw constantly suggests his theory through his method.

But even though the third act is dialectically structured, the cyclical nature of the whole of human history is explicitly suggested by the Devil and assented to by Don Juan: "An epoch is but a swing of the pendulum; and each generation thinks the world is progressing because it is always moving." And in Tanner's view, what has so far been applauded in history is just "goose-cackle about Progress." This tendency toward cyclical rhythm is evident in the play as a whole, but it is strongly counterbalanced by dialectical rhythm, especially in the dream symposium, which reveals the mythic deep structure most forcefully. In contrast, the surface realism of the other three acts—where the action is more cyclically oriented—conceals the play's mythic nature through the addition of specific incidents, psychologically plausible motivations and a setting in the very mundane world of Victorian England. Shaw's real joke, therefore, is that he has indeed given the world a Don Juan *play*, not merely a Don Juan *scene*.

In the dream symposium in hell, Shaw presents a void peopled with incorporeal characters. This conscious movement away from the particulars of a given scene is a method of universalizing, since the action is abstracted from concrete time and place, thereby creating a zone in which action becomes ceremony, and actors, archetypes. Instead of Tanner, Ann, Mendoza and Ramsden, Ann's guardian, we find hero, goddess, the Devil and Holdfast, the guardian of the status quo. Hell, with its ease of access to both heaven and earth, becomes, in effect, Shaw's satiric version of a sacred center of the universe. Using ritual techniques, Shaw expresses the philosophy of Creative Evolution, which becomes inclusive in that the major planes of experience are accounted for—the biological, the spiritual and the psychological. The hope for a superman is but another of the messianic visions that characterize many religions and which, like Creative Evolution, look forward to future generations. This belief in a messiah can also be correlated with Shaw's socialistic fervor since, as Eliade points out, "at the end of the Marxist philosophy of history lies the age of gold of the archaic eschatologies."

The age of gold Shaw envisions is possible only through evolution in a future time suggested by the play but not encompassed by the action. Thus, in order to make Creative Evolution dramatically viable, Shaw uses the Don Juan legend as his preeminent vehicle. Frequently occurring in musical and literary treatment, the legend has been raised to the level of myth through its reappearance apart from any historical context. Though our popular culture bears witness to the degeneration of many mythic patterns, these same patterns may revivify and function creatively for man. The changing character of Don Juan in treatments subsequent to Tirso de Molina's *El Burlador de Sevilla* attests to the vigor of this myth. The reason for this vigor is clear, for the myth expresses man's perennial longing for an earthly paradise. But the mundane form of the Don Juan myth does not disguise its similarity to Shaw's myth of Creative Evolution, which also has an earthly paradise as goal. Both Creative Evolution and the Don Juan myth express the same basic human desires, differ though they may in form and level of spirituality. In addition, the appropriateness of the Don Juan myth to Shaw's dramatic needs lies in its protean nature, evidenced in the multiple transformations undergone by the Don Juan figure in succeeding works of art. More important than the specific transformations the unfolding legend provides is the very fact of change itself. Thematically, the fluid Don Juan myth becomes a favorable milieu for Creative Evolution: the evolving form of the sexually based Don Juan myth becomes intimately associated with Shaw's evolutionary myth, which depends on the power of sexual energy for its ultimate triumph. Consequently, the legend—which Shaw alluded to in his first novel through the hero Don Juan Lothario Smith, and later in the short story "Don Giovanni Explains" through the ghost of Don Juan—becomes in *Man and Superman* the vehicle through which Shaw communicates his cosmic philosophy. And the Don Juan character, which has evolved and will evolve in yet uncreated works of art, becomes the logical complement to the elusive and variable Ann.

Against this mythic background, the woman-dominated action becomes at once more comic and also more necessary. It is more comic because, though the frivolity masks the profundity, the cosmic nature of Ann's very mortal quest calls forth the indulgent laughter of the kind that concludes the play. We look at the surface structure and witness, amused, a moral, unmarried woman, afraid to flout convention openly, yet determined to usurp the male prerogatives of choice, chase and capture. Ann's far from original actions place her in a long line of heroines from Shakespeare's Rosalind, as Shaw acknowledges in the Epistle Dedicatory, to Tennessee Williams's Maggie the Cat—women who *will* have their way. Ann's typicality, however, in no way supplants her archetypicality, which is based on the structural simplicity and range of her universal role. But the typicality of her modern role suggests that the role has undergone degeneration, thereby setting up an unrelieved comic tension in the play. Oblivious to this incongruity, Ann plays out her attenuated modern role against the awesome background her mythic precursors have erected.

The mythic background also makes the woman-dominated action more necessary, because the movement of the Life Force toward a more highly evolved human being requires the active participation of the female in capturing the male. If it is to serve Shaw's philosophical purpose, the Don Juan myth *must* be inverted. Of course, the inversion is apparent in both the romantic comedy and the dream symposium. Tanner's participation in a pattern that exactly imitates the acts of his ancestor thus endows with a ritualistic character his simultaneous fascination with and flight from Ann, while the act of repetition makes Tanner a contemporary of Don Juan in mythic terms.

Given this need for active women and, as a consequence, relatively passive men, Shaw's strict observance of the traditional man-woman / mind-body dichotomy is itself an inversion, since that dichotomy assumes the passivity of women and their corresponding domination by men. In examining this traditional phenomenon, J. C. Flugel observes that "there exists a very general association between the notion of mind, spirit or soul, and the idea of the father or of masculinity; and on the other hand between the notion of body or of matter (materia—that which belongs to the mother) and the idea of the mother or of the feminine principle." In general, the Victorians believed that women were passive. Faith in Woman's essential passivity encouraged Victorian men to relegate spiritual and moral concerns to her, thereby freeing the men to assume their aggressive and superior roles as captains of industry.

Shaw ignores this contemporary division in male-female roles in favor of the ahistorical view so vehemently asserted by Nietzsche. Nietzsche's simplistic avowal that "everything in woman hath a solution—it is called pregnancy," however, is modified by Shaw's Schopenhauerian belief in will. Ann, heir to this will, is consequently endowed with certain aggressive tendencies popularly thought to be masculine. But, psychologically, this is not necessarily so, according to the twentieth-century symbolist J. E. Cirlot, who believes that Western man is currently "dominated by the feminine principle." Thus, in her unrelenting desire to have her way, Ann, the representative of the feminine principle, is the antithesis of the fondly held Victorian view of Woman martyred upon the wishes and demands of others. Yet Ann's willingness to sacrifice her life for her maternal duty delineates ultimately an emotional similarity to the most docile Victorian wife. The means may differ; the end is the same. And what we see is Ann's manipulation of the means available to her, a trait that marks her as an unmistakably Shavian character. Through this manipulation Ann emerges supreme in a way Tanner does not even approximate, since her instincts transcend her limited awareness, while Tanner's intellect is by definition inferior to that of the evolving superman and by nature less forceful than Ann's will.

Although she lacks the higher intellect the superman will supposedly possess, Ann is more than an instrument of the Life Force, for she becomes identified with the essence of Creative Evolution itself. Her elusive nature, ever-changing, ever-various, is symbolic of the unending process involved in Creative Evolution. Such a process defies easy definition. Therefore the characters around her are able to discriminate only those qualities they most desire in a woman or expect to see. To Ramsden she is an inexperienced young woman; to Tanner she is a predatory animal; to Octavius she is a romanticized Earth Mother. These views of Ann all rely on the conception of Woman implicit in the mythic deep structure, making increasingly apparent the truth of Shaw's seeming jest in the Epistle Dedicatory: "every woman is not Ann; but Ann is Everywoman."

Ironically, it is Octavius's view of Ann that synthesizes these qualities and most directly refers to a mythic origin: "To Octavius [the stage directions assert] she is an enchantingly beautiful woman in whose presence the world becomes transfigured, and the puny limits of individual consciousness are suddenly made infinite by the mystic memory of the whole life of the race to its beginning in the east, or even back to the paradise from which it fell." The effete Octavius, because of his excessively romantic disposition an object of Shaw's satire and Tanner's pity, becomes a vehicle through which Shaw playfully incorporates mythic motifs; simultaneously, Shaw delights in Tanner's own romantically charged view of himself as *raisonneur* and Life Force advocate. The real humor is that Tanner, who warns Octavius of Ann, is ultimately vanquished by his own romantic temperament. When he recognizes imminent defeat, Tanner characteristically rationalizes his predicament by attributing to the Life Force his personal desires, and "renounc[ing] the romantic possibilities of an unknown future."

Plagued as he is by chronic pragmatic astigmatism, Tanner's perception of Ann can only be partial, and therefore distorted. Octavius's view is also distorted, as long as it is limited to the transfiguring enchantment of a beautiful woman, but the implications of his view are far richer. Paradoxically, the illusion-blinded Octavius sees more of the total configurative pattern surrounding Ann than Tanner, who prides himself on his perception of the order of things. This pattern, which is not perceived in its totality by any single character, subsumes a startling array of roles: daughter, sister, virgin, temptress, bride and mother—all within the mythological role of Queen Goddess of the World, the archetypal goddess who consumes as well as nourishes. Ascribing this role to Ann implies both the humor inherent in all myth, as it perpetually renews itself in strange and marvelous forms, and Shaw's very special sense of the absurd. That the decorous Ann Whitefield, whose name suggests commonplace innocence and nubility, should rise, by means of her vitality, to genius and hence to godhead, is, of course, comically incongruous. But this very incongruity affirms the inexhaustible nature of the mythological experience, which is never naturalistic, but is rendered in fantastic and exaggerated shapes. From the broad comic viewpoint of joy in exuberant life, Ann as a large figure representing such life is eminently plausible. She is archetypal Woman, carrier of the Life Force, Shaw's embodiment of the Blakean credo of celebration: "Energy is eternal delight."

With Ann as goddess, and therefore lure and guide to the hero Tanner, comedy erupts as she tries to lead Tanner from *dianoia* to *nous*, from merely rational knowledge to the unifying wisdom possible only through determined will and faith. But Tanner, like many a mythic hero, does not know a goddess when he sees one. Consequently, he responds to Ann in a classic way, recognizing in her only the temptress, a role he disdains on intellectual grounds. Though Tanner is wonderfully unsuccessful in convincing Ann of anything, his limited view of her role has largely prevailed with the critics. What is amazing is the extent to which Ann's actions are defined through Tanner's labeling. It is the age-old power ploy of manipulation through categorization. Not content to compare Ann to one or two familiar predatory animals, Tanner refers to her variously, but not necessarily imaginatively, as "cat," "boa constrictor," "lioness," "tiger," "bear," "spider," "bee," and "elephant." Ann, however, is merely amused as she becomes a veritable one-woman zoo. And we may wonder if Shaw has not *for once* overdone a good thing.

Yet Shaw has not arbitrarily chosen these unlikely animals only to allude outrageously to Ann's hunting instinct, as has been commonly assumed: these comic epithets playfully underscore a wide range of Ann's attributes. In mythic lore, the lioness is held to be a symbol of the *Magna Mater*, while the queen bee is associated with both the mother goddess and the Virgin Mary. These three roles represent the extreme of views held by Tanner, Octavius and Ramsden, respectively. Similarly, the creativity, aggressiveness and illusion associated with the spider are traits that Ann exhibits as she pursues and persuades, as much as she exhibits the strength and powerful libido which tradition accords the elephant.

But it is the snake epithet that occurs most often, at least four times. In addition, there is the stage business of the feather boa coiled around Tanner's neck. Inextricably identified with Eve—with whom Ann is linked in the stage directions—the snake more than any other creature symbolizes the feminine principle. With its sensuous movements, tenacious strength and glittering coloration, the snake is closely allied to the alluring, vividly garbed Ann, whose power lies in her insinuating charm, which Tanner suggests when he labels her "my dear Lady Mephistopheles." Even Ann's facile movement from young innocent to chaste seductress to unscrupulous huntress is reflected in the snake image, bringing to mind the periodic shedding of skin that gives the snake the appearance of becoming a new and different creature. Once again the evolutionary process, with which Ann is clearly associated, is suggested. Moreover, the snake is regarded as a symbol of energy, thereby epitomizing one of Ann's essential qualities.

The importance of the animal imagery extends beyond these affinities to Ann's portraiture. In the symbolic interpretation that makes the play's deep structure meaningful, the majority of the animals are considered lunar animals. The significance of the lunar relationship increases when we note that the cat (sacred to the Egyptian goddess of marriage), the bear (companion to Diana), and the tiger (symbolic of darkness and Dionysus) all have specific associations with the moon in various mythologies. In addition, there is an implied connection between these animals and basic instincts which preclude spirituality. Ann's powerful instincts and indifference to certain intellectual and spiritual qualities should therefore be viewed within the implied metaphorical framework of the moon, perennially evocative of desire.

The aptness of the lunar metaphor is readily apparent. Thought to be passive because it reflects the sun's light, the moon is traditionally associated with the feminine principle. Indeed, the physiological functioning of the female is viewed as in some way dependent on the fertility-controlling lunar cycle. Consequently, the additional feminine qualities of maternal love and protection are attributed to the moon, even while its half-light creates an aura suggestive of danger and the unconscious. These lunar qualities surface in Ann's inability to explain her motives consciously. Nevertheless, she risks all to be wife and mother, even "perhaps death." More pointedly, Shaw's portrait of Ann is directly consistent with the major characteristic imputed to the moon, a felicitous ability to appear as both the chaste Diana and the sorceress Hecate. And the incessant modifications in its apparent shape that the moon undergoes are reflected in Ann's constant role-changing.

Ann's characterization, which is immediately exhibited in the play's surface structure and greatly affects the progress of the action, is, therefore, actually dependent on the mythic substructure. The entire surface structure itself is in fact regulated by the deep structure, which determines Ann's centrality and her metaphorical identification with the moon. For this identification to be in any way conclusive, the body of lunar myths must be taken into account, and they must effectively increase our understanding of the play.

Eliade has shown "the importance of lunar myths in the organization of the first coherent theories concerning death and resurrection, fertility and regeneration, [and] initiation." This is especially significant for *Man and Superman*, since the play's structure expresses Shaw's satiric view of societal interpretations of a number of rites of passage—birth, death, marriage and initiation. The opening of act 1 is actually a mock celebration of death, as family and friends manipulate the legal will of the deceased Mr. Whitefield so they can assert their own personal wills. Octavius and Ramsden luxuriate in their sorrow, trade sentimental clichés and gravely discuss Ann's future. The bereaved daughter, beautifully dressed in black and violet silk, "which does honor to her late father," and expressing all the proper sentiments, uses the occasion to begin to have her way. This terrestrial view of death is reflected in Doña Ana's conventional views in the opening scene in hell, integrating the surface structure of the dream symposium with the romantic comedy. Don Juan, believing all such conventions to be masks of reality, disdains the code of conduct, just as Tanner ignores it. But both Ann and Doña Ana instinctively eschew death, being supremely concerned with life.

Dialectically balancing this mock celebration of death is the comic mourning of birth. The disclosure that the supposedly unmarried Violet Robinson is pregnant initiates the parody. In defending Violet, Tanner preaches the triumphant language of the Scriptures, strengthening the scene's ritualistic ties: " 'Unto us a child is born; unto us a son is given.' " This passage is paralleled by the segment in hell in which the superman subject is constantly implied as Don Juan speaks "of helping Life in its struggle upward." The possibility of change, which is evidenced in the restlessness of the characters, becomes all-important in hell's changeless environment. Don Juan wants to exchange his infernal residence for a heavenly one; the Statue wants to trade the tedium of heaven for the illusion of romance that hell provides; and the Devil claims to move back and forth between the two realms, citing the Book of Job as evidence. Implied in the desire for change are natural and supernatural birth, which are alluded to or examined in both structures of the play. Thus, in the romantic comedy, Tanner confesses to the birth of moral passion within him. Thematically, this description of the origin of Tanner's moral consciousness prefigures the discussion in hell, which posits the need for the advent of an intellectually superior being, by drawing attention away from the merely biological aspect of birth.

Having inverted the conventional rituals surrounding death and birth, Shaw inverts the rituals of wooing, with Ann pursuing Tanner on earth and Doña Ana pursuing a father for the superman: "For though by her death she is done with the bearing of men to mortal fathers, she may yet, as Woman Immortal, bear the Superman to the Eternal Father." Shaw thus reinterprets, for the purposes of his myth, essential parts of the cycle of human experience, which satirically illuminate the community he is portraying.

But beneath the surface structure, Tanner moves through a series of adventures, which form a necessary prelude to his marriage to Ann. These adventures, though comic, are akin to the journey of the mythic hero as he is initiated into the mysteries of life. As hero, Tanner implicitly embodies those qualities complementary to Ann's lunar nature. Because of his courageous and vigorous renewal of the world order, the hero has frequently been considered a human analogue of the sun, the sun itself being allied with the masculine principle. In addition, the sun early was identified with the rational intelligence and, hence, with the philosopher. Tanner's characterization, of course, relies on his philosophical aspirations and his faith in the rational intelligence. The single god, however, that is most closely associated with the virtue of judgment is not Apollo, as might be expected. Rather it is Jupiter. The stage directions introducing Tanner are explicit. Not only is he "prodigiously fluent of speech, restless, excitable" with "snorting nostril and . . . restless blue eye," but he also has an "Olympian majesty," suggesting "Jupiter rather than Apollo." Tanner's belief that strength of judgment should forge destinies is immediately suggested by the analogy, since tradition grants Jupiter this mythical power. Despite such power, it was his union with the Great Goddess that made Jupiter sacred, although—unlike many sky gods—marriage did not diminish his ability to guarantee universal order. Tanner's view of marriage as a muffin-like affair may not be the *only* possibility.

These implicit mythic ascriptions to Tanner prepare us for his nightlong journey into hell, a journey, according to mythic lore, the sun makes each night. Tanner's metaphorical descent into his unconscious is a journey through the labyrinth of his own disordered thoughts and emotions, as he seeks through his pilgrimage an initiation into "absolute reality," what can be called the mystic center of his spirit. This journey takes place largely within the third act. The call to adventure is instigated by Ann's insistence, shocking to the blustering Tanner, that they motor across Europe together. "Wildly appealing to the heavens," Tanner heeds the call, which indicates that he is on the threshold of new experience. Just as Goethe's Mephistopheles guides Don Juan's "cousin Faust," Tanner's supernatural guide is the Devil himself, who will attempt to win over the life-worshiping Tanner-Don Juan.

The Devil is first encountered as the bandit leader, Mendoza. His band of brigands, living in the seclusion of the Sierra Nevadas, is a transmutation of the dangerous creatures of mythology found in isolated places. Whether generally described as dragons, ogres or monsters, or specifically defined like Pan and his satyrs or like the enticing Sirens—all these creatures represent tests for the hero who enters their domain. The kind of geographical isolation in which such creatures are found is fertile ground for the unconscious to project its fantasies, so that frequently in mythology the hero crosses the first threshold into a mysterious zone through a dream.

Tanner's dream—framed by Mendoza's suggestion that "this is a strange country for dreams," and his later question, "Did you dream?"—follows an ancient pattern. As the dream begins, the scene fades into the extraordinary world of hell, which functions as a sphere of rebirth attainable only after self-annihilation and hence metamorphosis have occurred. During the course of the dream, Tanner moves back in time to become his ancestor Don Juan, who, paradoxically, is more advanced spiritually than he. Don Juan's commentary, largely a response to Doña Ana, externalizes the long woman-dependent educational process he has undergone. As a result of this commentary, we glimpse his unrevealed soul, which, in the fashion of a medieval morality play, becomes the prize multiple adversaries vie for. Viewed from the standpoint of the play as a whole, Tanner articulates through his dream those psychological and intellectual obstacles which impede his struggle toward enlightenment. His reincarnation as Don Juan leads to his subsequent rebirth as a more mature individual, one better able to assume the responsibilities of fatherhood and the vagaries of life with Ann.

That this assumption of parental obligation is a *raison d'être* for the dream symposium is evident from the commentary in hell. There such subjects as civilization, morality and progress appear to be disparate. But actually all of the subjects are related to those posited in the romantic comedy—love, marriage, sex and Woman—since all contribute to an understanding of Creative Evolution, through which fathers are fashioned and, ultimately, supermen ascend. The theme of Creative Evolution is further reinforced by the physical and spiritual metamorphoses the characters undergo in hell, where the setting transforms earthly time and space. In the process of metamorphosis, the characters lose extraneous personal traits exhibited in the romantic comedy, leaving only the quintessential qualities necessary for the creation of the superman, fertility and energy in Doña Ana, and intellectual and spiritual striving in Don Juan. Doña Ana and Don Juan typify these qualities—or type them in the nineteenth-century vitalist sense—placing them in the line of inheritance. The entire play moves toward this evolutionary change that is at once supremely symbolized by Ann in her many guises and championed by Tanner-Don Juan, for the mythological hero heralds the Life to Come.

Theme, philosophy, action and psychology intersect, all levels of dramatic action indicating that the flux of life can be integrated, assimilated and regenerated through the union of the world-embracing goddess-mother and the world-renouncing hero-saint. This union can occur only after Tanner, as hero, has traveled to the underworld and brought back the boon of his life-restoring private insight to the waiting community. Very often in myth, because the hero fails to return unaided or refuses to abandon the joy he has found, the society which he has left must seek him, as is true in Tanner's case. He cannot, as Don Juan, be allowed to find his contemplative bliss in heaven; he must be brought back to the earthly world of practical reality and coerced by Ann into enriching the social community.

To the mythic journey of the hero, the presentation of rites of passage and the identification of the characters with archetypal figures must be added a fourth element of the mythic deep structure—setting. The first two acts are set in the present of Victorian England, suggesting the beginning of a pattern of growth, whose mature fruit will be evident in the Spanish Sierras of act 4. But before that happens, act 3 moves toward spatial freedom, opening in the uncertain light of evening and therefore signaling uncertain space amid the inhospitable arid landscape of the Sierra Nevadas. Scattered patches of olive trees, Jupiter's sacred tree, impart an ancient and religious aura. The mountains dominate the action; Tanner refers to the "august hills," and much stage movement involves climbing or sitting on rock formations. The symbolism of the mountains foreshadows the movement into the void of hell, for "the Sacred Mountain—where heaven and earth meet—is situated at the center of the world."

It is not only in act 3, though, that the center of the world is suggested.

Again in act 4, the mountains overshadow the action. The universality of the action to ensue is indicated by the opening description of the setting which could "fit Surrey as well as Spain," except for the "Alhambra, the begging, and the color of the roads." But the little drama that Tanner and Ann could act out on English soil is elevated and made more inclusive by the presence of the Alhambra in the background. Taking its name from the red of its clay bricks, the Alhambra, by means of its color, symbolizes passion, blood, fire and sublimation. The dualism suggested by the opposition of passion and sublimation is specifically supported by the history of the Alhambra. This fortress palace was originally constructed in the thirteenth century by Moorish monarchs, who were expelled some two and a half centuries later. Soon after, the already damaged structure was partially demolished by the Spanish Charles V to make room for a Renaissance palace of Italian style. Ravaged in the early nineteenth century by Napoleon's army and then an earthquake, the building remained standing. Man's blood lust and his spiritual ascendancy through created art fuse in the history of the Alhambra, just as ages and cultures fuse in its design. These evidences of the best and worst of man's intentions, which are set against the expansive background of centuries, underscore the Alhambra's symbolic meaning and relate it to the "architectonic symbolism of the Center." Eliade observes that "every temple or palace—and, by extension, every sacred city or royal residence—is a Sacred Mountain, thus becoming a Center. Being an *axis mundi*, the sacred city or temple is regarded as the meeting place of heaven, earth, and hell."

As a center, the Alhambra reflects cosmic images, but it illuminates Tanner's earthly struggle as well. The building is dominated by the famed Fountain of the Lions, and it is the lion that is the animal most closely associated mythologically with the sun and the masculine principle, and therefore with Tanner. Also striking is the unusual architectural design, which includes the ubiquitous use of water in both static and dynamic forms, signifying death and rebirth. This strongly suggests that Tanner's encounter in hell has revitalized him in the manner of a religious discipline; his former self is annihilated as the result of the psychological rigor he has undergone, and a new life awaits him.

At the same time that the action moves toward new life, it expands outward into atemporality. Act 1 is set indoors, closed within Ramsden's study, which is itself a symbol of outmoded liberalism and narrow perspective. Act 2 moves outdoors to "the park of a country house." In act 3 the cultivated regions give way to an unknown mountainous zone, and finally to the timeless eternity of hell. The force of the atemporality of act 3 carries over into the fourth act, partially through the symbolism of the

Alhambra and partially through the hilly garden landscape. The setting stresses "a circular basin and fountain in the centre, surrounded by geometrical flower beds, gravel paths, and clipped yew trees in the genteelest order," from which steps lead to "a flagged platform on the edge of infinite space at the top of the hill." This extremely ordered landscape signals the return to the rational, conscious world, while the steps symbolize the spiritual evolution Tanner has achieved. The flagged stone platform functions as an *omphalos*, a ritualistic center, uniting heaven and earth and signifying the presence of the superhuman. Often the *omphalos* bears witness to a covenant—even such as will be made between Ann and Tanner. The fountain, imitative of the Alhambra's fountain, suggests the omnipresence of the Life Force and is situated at the absolute center of the sacred zone. Reinforcing the symbolism of the center of the world is the presence of the yew trees, since these trees are considered a particular symbol of immortality and regeneration. And the implicit greenness of vegetation and water supports the suggestion of fertility and the life process.

This movement into atemporality and regeneration, which the setting traces, crucially depends on the existence of the dream symposium, the movement corresponding to Jung's hypothesis on dreams. Summarizing Jung's concept, Campbell states that archetypal themes appearing in dreams "are best interpreted . . . by comparison with the analogous mythic forms. . . . Dreams, in Jung's view, are the natural reaction of the self-regulating psychic system and, as such, point forward to a higher, potential health, not simply backward to past crises." Thus Tanner's dream, which transposes a personal relationship into a universal fable of evolution and creation, powerfully affirms the possibilities for a regenerated society, even while it satirizes vice and folly. And Tanner, by means of the labyrinthine dream that has unfolded his hopes and beliefs, has simultaneously attained the center and knowledge of himself. Having journeyed successfully from hell, he has traveled the route Eliade shows the hero eternally traversing, "from death to life, from man to divinity." He has completed his initiation, becoming a worthy mate for Ann. Tanner may pun on being "sacrifice[d] . . . at the altar," still believing he is "scapegoat" and sacrificial lamb, as Ann works her "magic" with "siren tones," but the humor really lies in his wry realization that the Life Force is triumphant. Tanner cries out: "The Life Force. I am in the grip of the Life Force." Soon after, "the echo from the past," based on dialogue from the dream symposium, like the "echo from a former existence" which Ann earlier experienced, brings the dream of the third act directly into the romantic comedy: "When did all this happen to me before? Are we two dreaming?"

In terms of the play's deep structure, the promised marriage becomes a mystical marriage, which unites the contrary qualities of heaven and earth, sun and moon, representing Tanner's apprehension of life through Ann, who *is* life. This unique personal action of Ann and Tanner is so intimately connected with the community at large that only the sudden arrival of family and friends accomplishes the betrothal. The reluctant Tanner is finally brought into the social unit, the anticipated marriage ceremony serving to keep the community intact, thereby ostensibly reinforcing the status quo; however, the hoped-for birth of the superman, issuing from the union of Ann and Tanner, promises a new society rising above the morally archaic, absurdly flawed, human institutions of the present. The chorus of universal laughter attests to the transcendent nature with which life itself is endowed in vitalist philosophies. While Tanner protests that he is not a happy man, and Mendoza claims that life is a tragedy whether or not one gets one's heart's desire, the myth of Creative Evolution overcomes these petty tribulations, clothing Ann's uncertain fate as mother, and Tanner's pretensions, with the dark glory of a modern Divine Comedy.

And undoubtedly the quality of a Divine Comedy so permeates Ann's characterization that to perceive her in any shallow or less complex way is really not to perceive her at all. Once the essential relationship of the mythic deep structure to the surface comedy is revealed, many of the apparent problems and discrepancies in Ann's characterization fall away; indeed her portrait achieves a startling clarity of focus. Far more than merely a strong-willed young woman who overpowers a somewhat foolish bachelor, Ann, as Woman Incarnate in Shaw's dramatic version of evolutionary myth, becomes nothing less than the hope of the race in the movement toward a superman. Certainly Shaw's Everywoman is no less than the complete woman, the perfect realization of womanhood, what Kenneth Burke, after Aristotle, would call the *entelechialization* of woman. For there is that about Ann which can only be termed perfection—perfection of charm, of fascination, of endless complexity married to single-minded drive. Embodying all female biological drives in a plenary way, she is not merely the average woman with average instincts. Nor is she the stereotypical woman who is reduced to caricatured simplicity as mere predator or abortive mother-woman. She is archetypal Woman, whose role subsumes all roles. Biologically she may serve the species and socially she may seem to serve men, but psychologically she is free to woo and win as she chooses. And instead of Octavius, who plays at love and life and poetry, she chooses Tanner, who, infused with moral passion, can tell her he adores creation "in tree and flower, in bird and beast, even in you." Just as she rescues Tanner from his private inferno of self-doubt, thus enabling him to function unseparated from society, so she urges the passions in his soul and psyche to be expressed within the societal framework as he seeks order and renewal. Paradoxically identified with both the origin of life and the end toward which life aspires, Ann is a culminant figure, epitomizing an entire spectrum of related qualities and exemplifying Shaw's art of dramatic imitation in all the richness of its symbolizing and universalizing aspects.

Comedy and Dialectic

Nicholas Grene

Having completed *Captain Brassbound's Conversion*, the last of the *Plays for Puritans*, Shaw announced his (temporary) retirement from the theatre in a letter to Ellen Terry:

> And now no more plays—at least no more practicable ones. None at all, indeed, for some time to come: it is time to do something more in Shaw-philosophy, in politics & sociology. Your author, dear Ellen, must be more than a common dramatist.

However, writing *Man and Superman* was not so much a new departure for him, as the fulfilment of an ambition conceived before he had even begun his career as a "common dramatist." Already in 1889, explaining his abandonment of the novel, he described the new form he wanted to develop instead:

> Sometimes in spare moments I write dialogues; and these are all working up to a certain end (a sermon, of course) my imagination playing the usual tricks meanwhile of creating visionary persons &c. When I have a few hundred of these dialogues worked up and interlocked, then a drama will be the result—a moral, instructive, suggestive comedy of modern society, guaranteed correct in philosophic and economic detail, and unactably independent of theatrical considerations.

From *Bernard Shaw: A Critical View*. © 1984 by Nicholas Grene. Macmillan and St. Martin's Press, 1984.

This reads like a blueprint for *Man and Superman*. Nothing is more re-markable about Shaw than the clarity with which he could conceive such a project long before it was realised; one can almost believe that *Man and Superman* was not written until 1901–2 only because he has not enough "spare moments" to write it before then.

When his "comedy and philosophy" was published in 1903 it confirmed most critics in their opinion that Shaw was no dramatist. Max Beerbohm in the *Saturday Review* was representative: "This peculiar article is, of course, not a play at all. It is 'as good as a play'—infinitely better, to my peculiar taste, than any play I have ever read or seen enacted. But a play it is not." Yet, although Shaw had planned something "unactably independent of theatrical considerations," directed not towards any actual audience but a hypothetical "pit of philosophers," he was incapable of producing anything in dramatic form which was untheatrical. As he himself said, "no man writes a play without any reference to the possibility of performance," and the introduction of the motorcar must have been designed with a view to the *coup de théâtre* to be created on stage by its spectacular exit at the end of act 2. The performance of *Man and Superman* and *Don Juan in Hell* separately in 1905 and 1907, and productions of the entire work since, have proved that it is by no means unactable. Indeed Shaw felt that the play's very success on stage made it a partial failure in terms of what he had conceived. *Man and Superman*, he claimed in the Preface to *Back to Methuselah*, was "a dramatic parable of Creative Evolution" which had got lost in the brilliance of the comedy. "The effect was so vertiginous, apparently, that nobody noticed the new religion in the centre of the intellectual whirl-pool." Accordingly in *Back to Methuselah* he omitted the distractions and wrote a "cycle of plays that keep to the point all through."

Only the most hard-bitten and committed of Shavians would be pre-pared to accept that the more purely doctrinaire *Back to Methuselah* represents an improvement on the hybrid *Man and Superman*. The "metabiological pentateuch" does indeed "keep to the point all through" to a devastating degree. But the mixed form of "comedy and philosophy" in the earlier play remains problematic. To what extent is it one at the expense of the other—a Platonic dialogue masquerading as a play, as Beerbohm suggested, or an over-successful comedy with its success obscuring its philosophical purpose, as Shaw himself claimed? I would argue that it is neither, that the comedy and the philosophy interlock and interpenetrate all but perfectly. Indeed it seems to me that its very coherence, the unity of its conception and design, constitute its major limitation. Although Shaw never wrote a play quite like *Man and Superman* again, it is central to his work, and the analysis of its unique form is of crucial importance in assessing the nature of his comedy of ideas.

The homogeneousness of *Man and Superman* is striking considering the heterogeneousness of its origins. No play better illustrates Shaw's image of himself as a crow that has followed many ploughs, hopping "hungry and curious, across the fields of philosophy, politics, and art." In the Epistle Dedicatory to *Man and Superman* he lists a whole pantheon of artists and thinkers "whose peculiar sense of the world I recognise as more or less akin to my own" with the implication that they all influenced the play. Among major ideological sources are Schopenhauer, Nietzsche and Samuel Butler; among formal models may be counted Mozart, Plato and Blake, but critics have identified many other likely influences. The Shavian synthesis produced from this unlikely and diverse range of materials represents a triumph of building and blending skills.

I suggested [previously] that Shaw's object from early on in his career was to harness the energies of comedy. In *Man and Superman* he set out to identify those energies, to define them explicitly within the play. We have not a comedy plus a philosophy, but rather a comedy philosophised. It is generally agreed that one of Shaw's main sources for the play was the chapter entitled "Metaphysics of the Love of the Sexes" in Schopenhauer's *The World as Will and Idea*. From this he derived the notion that individual sexual attraction was in fact a manifestation of an instinctive impulse of the race. But Shaw followed Schopenhauer not only in the specific concept of love, but in the object of supplying a metaphysics for the sexual relationship. Schopenhauer introduces his chapter by remarking that love, the overwhelming concern of poets and dramatists through the ages, has never been seriously considered by philosophers. He claims to be establishing for the first time a metaphysics of sexuality. Shaw similarly wished to reveal the ideological underpinning which might be detected in the traditional treatment of love and marriage in comedy.

It is this purpose of supplying it with an ideology which is the outstandingly original feature of *Man and Superman* as love-comedy. For all the iconoclasm of a Don Juan who is the pursued rather than the pursuer, the comic action of *Man and Superman* is not in itself all that unorthodox. In most love-comedies, even the most romantic, there is an anti-romantic strain implied in the form itself. Love is seen as a blind force controlling the characters, and the comedian exploits the ironic disparity between the apparent individuality of feeling expressed by the lovers and the sense that such feelings are universal and impersonal. The bed-trick, Shakespeare's identical twins, are archetypal devices used to suggest the interchangeability of love-objects. Love, sex and marriage in comedy are parts of a more or less cynically viewed social ritual in which individual impulse works always towards ends which are none of its own. What Shaw identifies as the Life Force in *Man and Superman* is no more than the shaping natural providence implicit in the probable and improbable multiple marriages at the end of so many traditional comedies.

If the idea of a metaphysics for sexual attraction may be derived from Schopenhauer, however, the full theory developed in *Man and Superman* is not. For Schopenhauer, at least in the "Metaphysics of the Love of the Sexes," the highest type of love was expressed in the most fully mutual passion, though that passion when consummated was likely to end in unhappy marriage. In Schopenhauer it is the will of the man which meets the intellect of the woman. With Shaw it is the woman who exercises the will, her own and that of the Life Force, and man the intellectual who tries to escape from it. There were, no doubt, personal reasons for Shaw's insistence on this image of the battle of the sexes with the reluctant male and the female aggressor. In *The Philanderer* already, writing directly out of his own experience, he had developed the figure of the hunted philosopher/hero. But even acknowledging this idiosyncratic bias, John Tanner and Ann Whitefield are not fundamentally out of line with the lovers of traditional comedy. Tanner is the type of the comic figure who defies the power of love and must be humbled into marriage. Ann, superficially docile and conventional, in fact wily and disingenuous in pursuit of her love, corresponds to a certain type of comic heroine. Once again it is not the battle of the sexes in *Man and Superman* which differentiates it from other comedies but Shaw/Tanner's continuous theoretical commentary upon it.

Nietzsche takes over where Schopenhauer leaves off in the ideological structure of *Man and Superman*. If the English language owes the word "superman" to Shaw, Shaw owed the concept to Nietzsche. According to Schopenhauer the human species itself was infinite; anything beyond it was unthinkable. Indeed the perpetuation of the species which was the implacable object of the will to live manifested in sexual attraction was, for him, a source of despair. Shaw's Life Force may have been based on Schopenhauer's World Will, but its positive evolutionary character was shaped by Samuel Butler, and its ultimate goal was the Nietzschean superman. The revelation of the doctrine of the superman is the main aim of the dream interlude, *Don Juan in Hell*. It is the final philosophic plane which it is the function of the comedy to reach. There is no necessary connection between the idea of the Life Force as the motive power of sexual attraction, the duel of the sexes, and the concept of the superman. Yet Shaw welds them into a single ideological pattern. Both man and woman, John Tanner and Ann

Whitefield, must serve the Life Force. His reluctance, her aggression are essential attributes of their several roles: he as intellectual, as independent mind, strives to escape from the tyranny of physical love and the personal subjection of marriage; she as the principle of vitality must use him to fulfill her creative purpose. Both together are instruments in the evolution of the race. The individuality and intellectual aspiration which makes Tanner resist marriage is precisely what attracts Ann to him as the "father for the superman."

Shaw not only creates an ideological unity out of the most disparate strands of thought but he uses all his dramatist's gifts to integrate his philosophy with his comedy. The social comedy of acts 1, 2, and 4 works as the embodiment and expression of many of the play's ideas, while the discursive debate in Hell which makes up most of act 3 is controlled with a comedian's skills of pace and timing. In the main plot Shaw's strategy with his hero/spokesman was to make him a comic figure who is always right, and yet always contrives to get everything wrong. One of the funniest scenes in the play is Tanner's impassioned defence of Violet's supposedly unmarried pregnancy in act 1. Shaw uses the incident—brought in with cheerful lack of preparation or relevance—to hit off all the absurdities of the conventional attitude towards illicit sexuality.

> OCTAVIUS: But who is the man? He can make reparation by
> marrying her; and he shall, or he shall answer for it to
> me.
> RAMSDEN: He shall, Octavius. There you speak like a man.
> TANNER: Then you dont think him a scoundrel, after all?
> OCTAVIUS: Not a scoundrel! He is a heartless scoundrel.
> RAMSDEN: A damned scoundrel. I beg your pardon, Annie; but
> I can say no less.
> TANNER: So we are to marry your sister to a damned
> scoundrel by way of reforming her character! On my
> soul, I think you are all mad.

Tanner is given an eloquent speech in defence of unmarried motherhood. But all of this leads up to the comic revelation of Violet's marriage and her acerbic rejection of his championship:

> VIOLET [flushing with indignation]: Oh! You think me a wicked
> woman, like the rest. You think I have not only been
> vile, but that I share your abominable opinions. Miss
> Ramsden: I have borne your hard words because I knew
> you would be sorry for them when you found out the
> truth. But I wont bear such a horrible insult as to be

> complimented by Jack on being one of the wretches of
> whom he approves. I have kept my marriage secret for
> my husband's sake. But now I claim my right as a
> married woman not to be insulted.

Jack is left "in ruins," the victim of the traditional comic nemesis visited upon those who show excess enthusiasm or bravado.

And yet Jack, here and throughout the play, is right—at least he expresses an exaggerated and flamboyant version of his author's views. His identification of Ann as the husband-huntress, the agent of the Life Force, is of course correct; it is only his idea that her quarry is Octavius rather than himself which is mistaken. His great tirade against mothers in act 2 is a vehement denunciation of the fashionable marriage-market:

> Oh, I protest against this vile abjection of youth to age! Look
> at fashionable society as you know it. What does it pretend to
> be? An exquisite dance of nymphs. What is it? A horrible proces-
> sion of wretched girls, each in the claws of a cynical, cunning,
> avaricious, disillusioned, ignorantly experienced, foul-minded
> old woman whom she calls mother, and whose duty it is to
> corrupt her mind and sell her to the highest bidder.

But he is so carried away with his indignation that he issues what he intends to be a merely rhetorical invitation to Ann to defy mother and convention by driving across Europe with him, and finds himself promptly and devastatingly accepted. Many critics have argued that the comic treatment of Tanner makes our reaction to his ideas an ironical one. I feel rather that Shaw's object is to make us laugh at the speechifying, not necessarily at what the speeches say. Tanner the thinker who yet cannot see where his thought may be taking him in the real world is not only a stock comic type—the astronomer who falls into the pit—but an illustration of Shaw's doctrine of the artist-man who must submit to the practical will of the woman.

The dream debate in Hell, the most explicitly philosophical part of the play, is in fact a *jeu d'esprit* put to extraordinary Shavian ends. Its tone is that of an eschatological joke. It combines schoolboyish irreverence with the reassuring comic bathos of discovering that life after death is quite a comfortable affair. We laugh as Doña Ana is disabused of her conventional notions of Heaven and Hell, angels and harps, devils and torments. There are mischievous cracks at the great literary images of the underworld and the afterlife. The Devil describes the misconceptions of his kingdom derived from two of the greatest fools that ever lived, an Italian and an Englishman. The Italian described it as a place of mud, frost, filth, fire, and venomous serpents: all torture. This ass, when he was not lying about me, was maundering about some woman whom he saw once in the street. The Englishman described me as being expelled from Heaven by cannons and gunpowder; and to this day every Briton believes that the whole of his silly story is in the Bible.

He cites the Book of Job as evidence of the fact that, so far from being irrevocably banished from Heaven, he can visit it as often as he wants.

Shaw called himself "a pupil of Mozart in comedy much more than of any of the English literary dramatists." But *Don Giovanni* is used in *Man and Superman* almost wholly for purposes of parody, diversion, comic relief. For all Shaw's ingenious arguments in the Epistle Dedicatory, his Don Juan has little significant relation to Mozart's or anyone else's. Instead we get a series of running gags based on anticlimactic inversion of the characters and attitudes of the opera. After the dramatic music of the Commendatore, appears the very urbane statue who excuses himself from singing the part Mozart wrote for him, explaining that he is unfortunately a countertenor rather than a bass. The Commendatore and Don Juan, even the unseen Don Ottavio, much to Doña Ana's indignation, are very good friends in the afterlife. Don Juan's murder of the Commendatore is reduced to farce by the latter's insistence that he was the better swordsman and would have killed Don Juan but for an accident. These recurrent jokes are used to punctuate and puncture the long speeches of Juan and the Devil which constitute the main substance of the dream debate. They serve as comic counterpoint to the Shavian dialectic.

Yet if Shaw disposes comically of the traditional supernatural view of the hereafter, it is to clear the ground for his own conception of salvation and damnation. He dispels the notion of Heaven and Hell as places of reward and retribution; goodness or evil meeting the recompense of happiness or pain do not come into it for Shaw. The Shavian distinction between salvation and damnation is a pure value judgment on different human states of mind in the here and now. It is the difference between living life as though it had a purpose and living it as though it had none beyond the enjoyment of life itself. To live for pleasure only, however sophisticated or apparently humane that pleasure may be, is to be damned, and an eternity of such pleasure-seeking is literally Shaw's idea of Hell. Heaven by contrast is not so much a place of pure and beatific contemplation as a place of directed thought. "To be in hell is to drift: to be in heaven is to steer." The debate between Juan and the Devil is between the affirmation and the denial of life, or rather the purposefulness of life. The Devil believes, in the great tradition of philosophical pessimism, that there is "nothing new under the sun." In "reform, progress, fulfilment of upward tendency" he sees "nothing but an infinite comedy of illusion." It is the ideological position with which Shaw quarelled all his life, most notably as he saw it represented in Shakespeare, and he uses Juan as his spokesman to set against it a teleology for man and the universe. For all the force of the Devil's great speech on man's love of death, Juan maintains with Shaw's full backing that there is purpose and meaning in the world, and that a Life Force works in and through man towards consummation in the superman.

Man and Superman is a single-minded play and, in spite of all its philosophical borrowings, there is no doubting that the single mind is Shaw's. The whole enormous work with all its appendages—Epistle Dedicatory and Revolutionist's Handbook—is essentially univocal, even monolithic. This is perhaps why it does not read like the modernist piece which it superficially resembles in form. In its ironic treatment of a great literary myth, in its philosophical underpinning, in its use of multiple modes, Man and Superman would seem to conform to the characteristic methods of modernism. One critic at least has tried to argue that it should be seen in the broad context of the symbolist movement of the late nineteenth and early twentieth centuries. But analogies with a work such as, say, Strindberg's Dream Play seem inappropriate. Shaw's play follows through with the cohesiveness and cogency of argument; it has none of Strindberg's apparent randomness of progression, his exploitation of irrational dream logic. There is nothing elliptical, nothing merely suggestive, nothing opaque in Man and Superman.

This is the more striking if one contrasts Shaw's methods and effects with those of writers whom he was more or less consciously following in different parts of the work, Plato and Blake. It seems likely that Shaw had read relatively little of Plato—maybe only The Republic—but he was someone who could make a little reading go a long way. There can be no doubt that in writing Man and Superman he had the Platonic model in mind; the dream in Hell he called "a Shavio-Socratic dialogue." As the Socratic dialectic led upwards towards the knowledge of the Forms, so Juan's debate with the Devil makes him take the road to a Heaven which is the home of "the masters of reality." This is perhaps the significance of a remark of Shaw's quoted in an earlier chapter, describing himself as "only a realist in the Platonic sense." Shaw's typical method of argument is Socratic insofar as it involves the initial disproof of conventionally held notions of truth to make possible progress towards ultimate philosophic truth. When Juan maintains that the only sort of man who has ever been happy is the philosophic man, he is echoing *The Republic*, and in some sense the Shavian superman is closer to Plato's philosopher king than he is to the Nietzschean *Übermensch*.

Shaw and Plato both believed in the technique of dialectic in the simple meaning of the term—argument through interlocutors as the basic method of truth-seeking. But for Plato there were dimensions of the truth which could not be adequately expressed through the debate of Socrates and his companions, and for these he had recourse to myth and parable. The change of mode from argument to myth in the Platonic dialogue suggests that beyond a certain point it is not possible to convey ultimate realities by direct but only by metaphoric discourse. Now *Don Juan in Hell* would seem to stand in the same relation to the rest of *Man and Superman* as, say, the myth of Er to *The Republic* or Diotima's parable of the origins and nature of love to *The Symposium*. It is conceived as a level beyond and outside the representational interplay of character and action. But unlike in Plato, it is not a significantly different type of discourse; instead it is merely a purer, more intense form of argumentative debate with Juan taking Tanner's Socratic role. The issues are made more abstract, more fully philosophic in *Don Juan in Hell*, but we never move into the indirect and symbolic mode represented by the Platonic myth. There is a continuous clarity, very undream-like, in the dream-sequence of *Man and Superman*.

Shaw's incapacity to find a different form of expression is also apparent in "The Revolutionist's Handbook." We might well expect that a pamphlet written by one of the dramatis personae, a book within the book, would be characteristically by the character rather than by his creator. But "The Revolutionist's Handbook" is just another of Shaw's Prefaces in masquerade—nearly every point made is a familiar Shavian hobby-horse illustrated elsewhere in his work. Perhaps it was as a final attempt to differentiate the "Handbook" from the expository harangue of the Epistle Dedicatory that he added the "Maxims for Revolutionists." It is here that Blake comes in. *The Marriage of Heaven and Hell* was clearly a favourite work with Shaw: he cites it as an influence on *The Devil's Disciple* and quotes it in the Epistle Dedicatory to *Man and Superman*. Blake was for him the founding father of the Devil's party, the tradition of nineteenth-century iconoclasm in which he included Ibsen, Nietzsche and no doubt himself. Robert Whitman's claim, therefore, that the "Maxims for Revolutionists" "are certainly modelled on and at times echoing Blake's 'Proverbs of Hell,' " is no doubt plausible enough. But what a difference between model and imitation. Shaw is scarcely at his best with something as pithy as the maxim anyway; his maxims are always turning into the periods and paragraphs which are his natural stylistic units. Where the maxims do come off, however, it is as satiric epigrams—"He who can, does. He who cannot, teaches"—and they range in tone from the cynicism of La Rochefoucauld to the flippancy of Wilde. The gnomic enigmatic quality of Blake's aphorisms, or indeed their sheer oddity, are qualities quite foreign to Shaw. The "Maxims for Revolutionists" are as pointed as everything else in *Man and Superman* and they are frequently the same points.

Part of the difficulty with *Man and Superman* is that there is not enough distinction between Shaw and his two avatars: Shaw *is* Tanner *is* Juan. It seems likely that Shaw did not, in the first instance, model Tanner on himself, in spite of Granville-Barker's cultivating recognisably G.B.S. make-up and business in the 1905 production. The introductory description of Tanner, it has been convincingly argued, shows that it was H. M. Hyndman, the Social Democratic orator and agitator, that was in Shaw's mind. Certainly Tanner, with his impulsiveness, his volatility, his all but mad energy, is a realised comic character in the first two acts, not a mere stand-in for Shaw. And Don Juan, although Tanner's alter ego, is distinguished from him: "A more critical, fastidious, handsome face, paler and colder, without Tanner's impetuous credulity and enthusiasm, and without a touch of his modern plutocratic vulgarity." The distinction is one that is apparent and effective in the theatre for those who have had a chance to see the play in its entirety. But the cooler, more austere Don Juan has in fact shed many of the non-Shavian characteristics of Tanner to become a more formidable spokesman for Shaw. Once the force of the debate takes hold on us, we lose the awareness of his separate identity as Don Juan. We only recognise that he is saying the same things, making the same arguments as Tanner did in acts 1 and 2, but making them more articulately, more cogently, without Tanner's comic extravagance. As a result we feel that this is what Shaw himself is driving at, through Tanner and through Juan.

Juan is, and is intended to be, more real than Tanner, in Shaw's Platonic sense of the word. With the dream in Hell the stage is cleared of supporting characters, motor-cars and brigands, the inessential props of the main plot, to make way for the "omnipresent nothing" against which the debate is set. Four voices are enough to argue out the ideological heart of the matter. But after that debate, to return to Tanner and the rest, the Strakers, the Violets and Malones, the cars and the brigands, is to feel that this *is* what Shaw called it, "a trumpery story of London life." If in the dream in Hell we sense that we have arrived where Shaw was taking us, the surrounding comedy begins to look like a merely factitious contraption to get us there. The characters of the main plot seem tedious and trivial by contrast with the bravura performers of the dream-sequence. The conventional thickening up of comic complications before the dénouement—the arrival of the Irish-American Malone Senior, the incorporated company of brigands Mendoza Ltd—appear feeble and facetious excrescences.

Act 4 is by far the least satisfactory part of *Man and Superman*, to some extent because the comedy looks artificial and contrived once what it was contrived for has been revealed. But it also suffers from the ideological explicitness of the comedy itself. This explicitness seems less obtrusive in the earlier acts of the play. The first love-scene between Ann and Tanner in act 1 is amusing because of his ironic lack of awareness of her intentions. There is a comic interplay between his enunciation of his ideas, his account of the development of his moral independence, and the reactions of Ann, hearing only what interests her, seizing any opening to undermine that boasted independence. We laugh at Tanner expatiating on theories of courtship without knowing that he is providing an illustration of his theories himself. The effect in the big scene between Ann and Tanner in act 4, when he *is* aware of what is happening, is quite different. The combined role of theoretical commentator and unwilling participant then becomes an awkward one. "We do the world's will, not our own. I have a frightful feeling that I shall let myself be married because it is the world's will that you should have a husband." The awkwardness here is partly a stylistic one; the colloquial lightness of tone in "I have a frightful feeling that I shall let myself be married" brands as pretentious the talk about the "world's will." And yet Shaw believes in the "world's will"—the whole play has been set up to show its action. There is a similar problem with a joke about the Life Force later on:

> ANN: . . . Why are you trying to fascinate me, Jack, if you
>   dont want to marry me?
> TANNER: The Life Force. I am in the grip of the Life Force.
> ANN: I dont understand in the least: it sounds like the Life
>   Guards.

Do we laugh at this, and if so is our laughter directed against Ann's anti-intellectualism or Tanner's pontificating?

It has been argued that in the semi-ironic treatment of Tanner, Shaw was expressing an awareness of his own absurdity, a sceptical acknowledgement of the limitations of his own ideas as applied to the real world.

But if that was indeed his aim, the hybrid form of *Man and Superman* makes it impossible for him to bring it off. Comedy is traditionally hostile to theory; a whole category of its butts—the schoolmaster, the pedant, the doctor, the lawyer—are theorists humiliated by the pragmatic force of experience. To some extent Tanner can be aligned with them, and Ann's puncturing attitude towards his grandiose theorising—"I am so glad you understand politics, Jack: it will be most useful to you if you go into parliament"—is standard comic debunking. But, particularly after the dream in Hell, we are also aware that Shaw believes in Tanner's ideas, however inflatedly he may put them, that they represent as near to Juan's ultimate heavenly reality as it is possible for a limited human character to get. As so often in Shaw's work, the nature of comic truth and the nature of a dialectically established would-be absolute truth are incompatible.

Shaw's explicitness in relation to the comic pattern in *Man and Superman* comes across as a want of artistic tact. Of such tact, a fine example is the reticence of Hippolyta's comment on the midsummer night's dreams, in response to Theseus' speech "The lunatic, the lover, and the poet":

> But all the story of the night told over,
> And all their minds transfigur'd so together,
> More witnesseth than fancy's images,
> And grows to something of great constancy;
> But, howsoever, strange and admirable.

There is indeed more meaning in the dreams of the lunatic, the lover and the poet than Theseus will allow, but Shakespeare will go no further than hinting with Hippolyta that such meaning exists. The integrity of the self-deprecating form of the midsummer night's dream is preserved from explanation or exegesis. Shaw in *Man and Superman* is not content with showing us the comic pattern, he must explain it as well. The self-consciousness of the interpretation seems embarrassing and out of place, particularly in the context of the final love-scene, if such it may be called. The relationship between Tanner and Ann appears false not because, to quote Judge Brack, "people don't do things like that," but because in comedy at least, people don't say things like this:

> ANN: Well, I made a mistake: you do not love me.
> TANNER [*seizing her in his arms*]: It is false: I love you. The Life
>   Force enchants me: I have the whole world in my arms
>   when I clasp you. But I am fighting for my freedom, for
>   my honor, for myself, one and indivisible.

Shaw's habitual difficulty in writing convincing dialogue for his lovers is here increased by his need to expound the significance of their love and love in general.

Man and Superman is an extraordinary *tour de force*. If one has any feeling for Shaw at all, one cannot withhold admiration for its inventiveness, its audacity, its combination of skill and stamina. Though in many ways a ramshackle construction, a loose and baggy monster in play-form, it is amazingly ingenious in the integration of its disparate elements. The debate in Hell represents a high-point in Shaw's dramatic rhetoric, so that for all the abstractness of its issues and its apparently static form, it compels concentrated attention in the theatre. Yet locked as it is into its own idiosyncratic form, the whole work seems curiously without resonance and without depth. Its relentless unity of tone and clarity of exposition leave no room for the organic development of form and meaning. It is autonomous, self-validating, remote ultimately from any real experience, even the deliberately distorted experience of comedy. The stereotyped characters of traditional comedy are representatives of universal patterns which implicitly supply significance. Shaw, in making his comic figures articulate their own significance, or rather having John Tanner articulate for all of them, produces an effect of alienating artificiality. *Man and Superman* is in one sense brilliantly successful in marrying comedy with philosophy, but as a work of art it fails ultimately by virtue of its very articulateness.

Chronology

1856	Born on July 26, in Dublin, Ireland.
1876	Moves to London in the hopes of professional advancement and becomes a small-time journalist.
1879	Hired by the Edison Telephone Company and completes his first novel, *Immaturity*.
1880	Writes a second novel, *The Irrational Knot;* joins the Dialectical Society.
1881	Becomes a vegetarian in an attempt to cure migraine headaches and takes lessons in boxing. Writes *Love Among the Artists*.
1882	Converts to socialism and completes his best novel, *Cashel Byron's Profession*.
1884	Falls among the Fabians; *An Unsocial Socialist* is serialized.
1885	Father dies.
1886–88	Works as an art critic and music critic for various journals.
1889	Publishes *Fabian Essays*.
1890	Begins work as a music critic for *The World;* lectures to the Fabian Society on Ibsen.
1891	Publishes *The Quintessence of Ibsenism*.
1892–93	*Widower's Houses, The Philanderer, Mrs. Warren's Profession.*
1894	*Arms and the Man, Candida.*
1895	Starts as drama critic for the *Saturday Review*. *The Man of Destiny, You Never Can Tell.*
1896	*The Devil's Disciple.*
1898	Gets married; *Caesar and Cleopatra, The Perfect Wagnerite.*
1899	*Captain Brassbound's Conversion.*
1903	*Man and Superman.*
1904	*John Bull's Other Island.*
1905	Visits Ireland; *Major Barbara.*

1906 Meets Ellen Terry; *The Doctor's Dilemma, Our Theatres in the Nineties.*

1908 *Getting Married.*

1909 *Misalliance, The Shewing-up of Blanco Posnet.*

1911 *Fanny's First Play.*

1912 *Androcles and the Lion, Pygmalion.* Friendship with Mrs. Patrick Campbell.

1914 *Common Sense about the War.*

1916–19 *Heartbreak House.*

1920 *Back to Methuselah.*

1923 *Saint Joan.*

1926 Receives the Nobel Prize for Literature—uses the prize money for the construction and publication of translations from Swedish literature.

1928 *The Intelligent Woman's Guide to Capitalism and Socialism.*

1929 *The Apple Cart.*

1931 *Ellen Terry and Bernard Shaw: A Correspondence.* Travels to U.S.S.R.

1932 *The Adventures of the Black Girl in Her Search for God.*

1933 Goes to America.

1934 *Collected Prefaces.*

1939 *In Good King Charles's Golden Days.*

1943 Wife dies.

1944 *Everybody's Political What's What.*

1950 Dies on November 13.

Contributors

HAROLD BLOOM, Sterling Professor of the Humanities at Yale University, is the author of *The Anxiety of Influence, Poetry and Repression,* and many other volumes of literary criticism. His forthcoming study, *Freud: Transference and Authority,* attempts a full-scale reading of all of Freud's major writings. A MacArthur Prize Fellow, he is general editor of five series of literary criticism published by Chelsea House.

ERIC BENTLEY is Katharine Cornell Professor of Theatre at the State University of New York at Buffalo. He has written extensively on contemporary drama. In addition to translating the work of Pirandello and Brecht he has directed such plays as Garcia Lorca's *The House of Bernarda Alba* and O'Neill's *The Iceman Cometh.* His own plays include *The Recantation of Galileo Galilei* and *Expletive Deleted.*

LOUIS KRONENBERGER was Professor of Theater Arts at Brandeis University. He was drama critic for both *Time* and *P.M..* His writings include essays on manners, a novel, a biography of Oscar Wilde, and drama criticism.

MARTIN MEISEL is Professor of English and Comparative Literature at Columbia University. One of our foremost critics of nineteenth-century drama, he is the author of *Shaw and the Nineteenth Century Theater* and *Realizations: Narrative, Pictorial, and Theatrical Arts of the Nineteenth Century.*

FREDERICK P. W. McDOWELL is Professor of English at the University of Iowa. He is the author of *Poet as Critic, Ellen Glasgow and the Ironic Art of Fiction,* and critical studies of Joseph Conrad and Virginia Woolf.

LOUIS CROMPTON is Professor of English at the University of Nebraska. He is author of *Shaw the Dramatist.* He writes extensively on homosexual literature and history; his most recent book is *Byron and Greek Love: Homophobia in 19th Century England.*

CHARLES A. BERST is Professor of English at the University of California at Los Angeles. He is the author of *Bernard Shaw and the Art of Drama* and editor of *Shaw and Religion*.

MAURICE VALENCY is Emeritus Professor of Dramatic Literature at Columbia University and Director of Academic Studies at Julliard. He has written extensively on modern drama and is the author of *In Praise of Love: An Introduction to the Love Poetry of the Renaissance* and the novel *Ashby*.

SALLY PETERS VOGT writes on Shaw and modern drama.

NICHOLAS GRENE is Fellow and Director of Studies in Modern English at Trinity College, Dublin. In addition to a critical study of Shaw, he has written *Shakespeare, Jonson, Molière: The Comic Contract* and *Synge: A Critical Study of the Plays*.

Bibliography

Adams, Elsie B. "Bernard Shaw's Pre-Raphaelite Drama." *PMLA* 81 (1966): 428–38.

Albert, Sidney P. "Bernard Shaw: The Artist as Philosopher." *Journal of Aesthetics and Art Criticism* 14 (1956): 419–38.

Bab, Julius. *Bernard Shaw*. Berlin: Fischer, 1926.

Barnett, Gene A. "Don Juan's Hell." *Ball State University Forum* 11, no. 2 (1970): 47–52.

Bentley, Eric. *Bernard Shaw, 1856–1950*. Amended ed. New York: Laughlin, 1957.

Bermel, Albert. "Jest and Superjest." *Shaw Review* 18 (1975): 57–68.

Berst, Charles A. *Bernard Shaw and the Art of Drama*. Urbana: University of Illinois Press, 1973.

Blanch, Robert J. "The Myth of Don Juan in *Man and Superman*." *Revue des Langues Vivantes* 33 (1967): 158–63.

Brown, Ivor. *Shaw in His Time*. London: Nelson, 1965.

Burton, Richard. *Bernard Shaw: The Man and the Mask*. New York: Holt, 1916.

Carpenter, Charles. "Notes on Some Obscurities in the 'Revolutionist's Handbook.' " *Shaw Review* 13 (1970): 59–64.

Chesterton, G. K. *George Bernard Shaw*. Dramabook ed. New York: Hill, 1956.

Colbourne, Maurice. *The Real Bernard Shaw*. New York: Philosophical Library, 1949.

Crompton, Louis. *Shaw the Dramatist*. Lincoln: University of Nebraska Press, 1969.

Dickson, Ronald J. "The Diabolian Characters in Shaw's Plays." *University of Kansas City Review* 26 (1959): 145–51.

Dukore, Bernard F. *Bernard Shaw, Director*. Seattle: University of Washington Press, 1971.

Ervine, St. John. *Bernard Shaw: His Life, Work, and Friends*. New York: Morrow, 1956.

Gibbs, A. M. *The Art and Mind of Shaw: Essays in Criticism*. London: Macmillan, 1983.

Grene, Nicholas. *Bernard Shaw: A Critical View*. London: Macmillan, 1984.

Hamon, Augustin. *The Twentieth Century Molière: Bernard Shaw*. Eden & Cedar Paul. New York: Stokes, 1916.

Henderson, Archibald. *Bernard Shaw: Playboy and Prophet*. New York: Appleton, 1932.

Holt, Charles L. "Mozart, Shaw and *Man and Superman.*" *Shaw Review* 9 (1966): 2–14.

Hoy, Cyrus. "Shaw's Tragicomic Iron." *Virginia Quarterly Review* 47 (1971): 56–78.

Hugo, Leon. *Bernard Shaw: Playwright and Preacher.* London: Methuen, 1971.

Irvine, William. *"Man and Superman,* A Step in Shavian Disillusionment." *Huntington Library Quarterly* 10 (1947): 209–24.

Joad, C. E. M., ed. *Shaw and Society: An Anthology and a Symposium.* London: Odhams, 1951.

Kaye, Julian B. *Bernard Shaw and the Nineteenth-Century Tradition.* Norman: University of Oklahoma Press, 1958.

Kronenberger, Louis, ed. *George Bernard Shaw: A Critical Survey.* Cleveland: World, 1953.

Leary, Daniel J. "Shaw's Use of Stylized Characters and Speech in *Man and Superman.*" *Modern Drama* 5 (1963): 477–90.

Mayne, Fred. *The Wit and Satire of Bernard Shaw.* New York: St. Martin's, 1967.

Meisel, Martin. *Shaw and Nineteenth-Century Theater.* Princeton: Princeton University Press, 1963.

Mencken, Henry L. *George Bernard Shaw: His Plays.* Boston: Luce, 1905.

Mills, Carl Henry. "Shaw's Superman: A Re-examination." *Shaw Review* 13 (1970): 48–58.

Morgan, Margery M. *The Shavian Playground: An Exploration of the Art of George Bernard Shaw.* London: Methuen, 1972.

Ohmann, Richard M. *Shaw: The Style and the Man.* Middletown, Conn.: Wesleyan University Press, 1962.

Rosenblood, Norman, ed. *Shaw: Seven Critical Essays.* Toronto: University of Toronto Press, 1971.

Stamm, Julian, L. "Shaw's *Man and Superman:* His Struggle for Sublimation." *American Imago* 22 (1965): 250–54.

Stockholder, Fred E. "Shaw's Drawing Room Hell: A Reading of *Man and Superman.*" *Shaw Review* 11 (1968): 42–51.

Strauss, Emil. *Bernard Shaw: Art and Socialism.* London: Gollancz, 1942.

Valency, Maurice. *The Cart and the Trumpet: The Plays of George Bernard Shaw.* New York: Oxford University Press, 1973.

Weintraub, Rodelle, ed. *Fabian Feminist: Bernard Shaw and Women.* University Park: Pennsylvania State University Press, 1977.

Wisenthal, J. L. "The Cosmology of *Man and Superman.*" *Modern Drama* 14 (1971): 298–306.

Acknowledgments

"The Theatre" by Eric Bentley from *Bernard Shaw* by Eric Bentley, © 1975 by Eric Bentley. Reprinted by permission of Proscenium Publishers.

"Shaw" by Louis Kronenberger from *The Thread of Laughter: Chapters on English Stage Comedy from Jonson to Maugham* by Louis Kronenberger, © 1952 and renewed 1980 by Louis Kronenberger. Reprinted by permission of Alfred A. Knopf, Inc.

"*Man and Superman* and the Duel of Sex" by Martin Meisel from *Shaw and the Nineteenth-Century Theater* by Martin Meisel, © 1963 by Princeton University Press. Reprinted by permission.

"Heaven, Hell and Turn-of-the-Century London" (originally entitled "Heaven, Hell and Turn-of-the-Century London: Reflections upon Shaw's *Man and Superman*") by Frederick P. W. McDowell from *Drama Survey* 2, no. 3 (February 1963). © 1963 by *Drama Survey*. Reprinted by permission of the University of Nebraska Press.

"Don Juan in Hell" (originally entitled "Man and Superman") by Louis Crompton from *Shaw the Dramatist* by Louis Crompton, © 1969 by the University of Nebraska Press. Reprinted by permission.

"The Play of Ideas in Act 3 of *Man and Superman*" (originally entitled "*Man and Superman*: The Art of Spiritual Autobiography") by Charles A. Berst from *Bernard Shaw and the Art of Drama*, © 1973 by the Board of Trustees of the University of Illinois. Reprinted by permission of the University of Illinois Press and the author.

"*Man and Superman*" by Maurice Valency from *The Cart and the Trumpet* by Maurice Valency, © 1973 by Maurice Valency. Reprinted by permission of Oxford University Press and the author.

"Ann and Superman: Type and Archetype" by Sally Peters Vogt from *Fabian Feminist: Bernard Shaw and Woman*, edited by Rodelle Weintraub, © 1977 by

145

The Pennsylvania State University. Reprinted by permission of Pennsylvania State University Press.

"Comedy and Dialectic" by Nicholas Grene from *Bernard Shaw: A Critical View* by Nicholas Grene, © 1984 by Nicholas Grene. Reprinted by permission of The Macmillan Press Ltd., the author, and St. Martin's Press.

Index